FORWARD BY JOHN MALOTT

SHIT GREAT LEADERS DO

A Compilation of Business Wisdom from Gurus, Game Changers and Gladiators

DR. BONITA PARKER

AN IMPRINT OF BP PUBLISHING

Shit Great Leaders Do

A Compilation of Business Wisdom from Gurus, Game Changers and Gladiators

BP Publishing
3485 Promenade Place, Suite 108
Waldorf, MD 20603

First Edition: September 2021

BP Publishing is a division of Bonita Parker Enterprises, Inc. The BP Publishing logo and tradename are solely owned by Bonita Parker Enterprises, Inc. The publisher is not responsible for websites (or their content) that are not owned by the publisher.

ISBN 978-0-692-19170-5
Library of Congress Control Number: Requested and pending distribution.

Printed in the United States of America.

DISCLAIMER OF LIMITED LIABILITY
Readers may find the information and teachings imparted in this book to be useful, however, the book is available with the understanding that the author, publisher, or its contributors are engaged in presenting any specific financial, career, legal, psychological, emotional, or health advice. Nor is the contents of this book deemed to be an analysis, recommendation, solution, diagnosis, prognosis, or solvent to any problem or issue held by the reader. It is recommended that any individual experiencing any of the aforementioned, seek assistance from a qualified professional before commencing any financial, career, health, change in their personal and/or business life, or embark on any of the teachings, suggestions, or methods as described in this book.

DEDICATION

To all new and aspiring entrepreneurs and business leaders ...

I hope that the knowledge imparted in this book will guide you in the direction of your dreams, help you achieve your desired goals, and propel you into a life unimaginable!

I believe that, once you reach your highest peak, you will then share your very own experiences, knowledge, and wisdom with others forthcoming. That's the great challenge – and that is how we build a legacy of leadership ...

Take your time, have fun on the journey, and always do it YOUR way!

Dr. Bonita Parker

Table of Contents

FOREWORD

"I don't have all the things that society says you're supposed to have to be successful. I don't have a college degree. I don't even have a high school diploma." ~ John Malott

When Dr. Parker reached out to me and asked me to write the Foreword for this book and share my thoughts and experiences related to entrepreneurship and leadership, I was completely honored. Based on my background, there was once a time where there was absolutely no way that I would have been considered for an opportunity like this, but it's these types of books that change lives – including my own. I can't help but go back to when I was introduced to my first book, *"How to Win Friends and Influence People?"* It opened me up to a world that I didn't know existed and truthfully, I don't know where I would be had I not read that book.

In this book, Carnegie talks about how the world opened to him and allowed him to move into another world by going after what he wanted and making what he had work for him. Similar to my success journey, he was incarcerated for 11 to 12 years and decided to go after a much better life other than the path of incarceration he was on. So, there's no question for me as to how important sharing this information is and being positioned to motivate other entrepreneurs. It all starts with information – imagine someone introducing you to something and you making the decision to either go forward or go backward. I hope that someone gets ahold of this book and says, *"Okay I'm deciding to change my course or change my direction because I want better for myself."*

My testament to this theory began back on July 4, 1993. My home was surrounded by the police, and while this wasn't the first time, it turned out this was the beginning of the end of the worse chapter of my life. I found myself locked up in Molokai County Jail and I'm sitting on the bullpen floor waiting for my trial. I had stitches on my head because before getting to the bullpen floor, I had an altercation with the police inside of my cell and they had beat me pretty good in that cell so needless to say, I sat there with a pounding headache and two things were playing over and over my mind while sitting on that bullpen floor. The first thing was something that I was told when I was 17 years old in a drug rehabilitation program after having a heart attack from smoking cocaine. There was a guy named Dave who was a counselor there. He used to say, *"A good man leaves an inheritance for his children's children."* I had no idea where it came from. I just remembered him talking about that. And as I sat on that bullpen floor, I kept thinking about my 2-year-old daughter, Lauren, who had witnessed me being physically removed from my house. She was screaming and crying and while she didn't know what was going on, I'll never forget the look in her eyes. It couldn't have been more than a couple of seconds, but it seemed like a lot longer, but at that moment, "A good man leaves an inheritance for his children's children" just kept replaying in my mind. And it was on that bullpen floor that I decided that I would never go through that or live that way again. I considered myself a loser. Yes, I was a criminal, drug addict, gang member – all these different things. But that's who I was and I decided that that was not who I would be, again. From that point on, I never did drugs again and I pursued entrepreneurship with the same passion and relentlessness that I pursued my drug addiction. So, the important thing that I learned quickly on my entrepreneurial journey was that we get what we go for.

Don't get me wrong, it wasn't easy. I didn't think that people like me would ever have a chance at success. It took me seven years to achieve success once I committed to the entrepreneurship process because nobody was opening doors for a high school dropout with a criminal history that couldn't speak well and unfortunately, in our society, it didn't matter if you've paid the price, people still slam doors in your face which makes it hard to evolve. I thank GOD for Dave giving me my first book and saying to me, *"okay maybe you're not gonna be an athlete, maybe you're not gonna be a college professor, but you could be the best businessperson you can be."* When he said that to me, it planted a seed that never went to waste. I pursued entrepreneurship with everything I had and unfortunately, it didn't happen fast. It took seven years to finally make $100k in a single year. In my first year as a full-time entrepreneur, I only made $4,000. Imagine people laughing and criticizing me, but I kept going. In my seventh year, I made $116,000, and the very next year it went over $220k, then one million, two million, and was ultimately a few hundred thousand dollars every single month. Of course, my life changed drastically, but it started from being so far behind, getting in a lot of trouble, and hanging in the wrong environments that eventually, the right people came into my life and started to nudge me in the right direction. People always see the end result, but what made me was all the foundational things that I've endured along the way.

Unfortunately, I've seen so many young entrepreneurs who did not know how to pivot from their mishaps and misfortunes. They make up all these excuses as to why they cannot be successful but if they just flip it in their minds that those are just useless excuses and they do not have to be a victim of their circumstance by asking themselves one simple question, *"How do I change these circumstances?" "How can I do this?"* Success is all about your mindset. Your own thinking can be the best – or the worst – deterrent to your success and affects the way you lead as an entrepreneur. You can't move beyond your circumstances if you don't fear the consequences of your actions.

Success for me happened when I decided to stop making excuses for my circumstances and implement my own success habits and principles that helped change the trajectory of my life. It was critical for me to have a life partner who not only was willing to walk to journey with me, but also hold me accountable for my actions when I was slipping. I start every single day in the same way which I think is critical to my success. One of the main things that I do with my incredible wife – without fail – is we start each day off with positive affirmations about ourselves and each other. That's a big part of strengthening our mindset. We also incorporate a gratitude exercise every single morning where we each produce three things that we're grateful for. Another important mind-strengthening activity that we do daily is read. We've really been focusing on the bible and Solomon's principle because as it relates to business, I wanted to learn principles from the person they said was the richest man that ever lived. *How interesting is that!* If you want to get rich if that's your goal – why not study the richest man that ever lived, that they said whose gold was worth trillion dollars? I have developed a habit of reading at least 15 pages of a good book every single day no matter what. Those seeds that were planted from receiving my first book helped me start a business and change the way I think about everything. For me, that's the foundation. And finally, as owners of a prominent health and wellness company, we make sure we are living by example so we incorporate a minimum of 2 hours of physical exercise into our daily routine.

My best advice to all entrepreneurs – whether you are seasoned, new, or aspiring, develop your success routine. Remember success starts in the mind. Once you reach each level of your journey, always humble yourselves by showing gratitude for the road traveled and the road ahead. *Ego is the worst enemy.* People will care for you while you're crushing it but secretly want to see you fail if you're an egomaniac. Not to mention, more doors will open for you if you're humbled.

My next piece of advice is to always be on a constant "development mission." A.B.L (always be learning). Your business is only going to grow to the level that you've grown. Too often I've seen where entrepreneurs only focus on one aspect of their lives while not realizing that they are all intertwined. You can't be successful in business if you aren't successful in your personal life. Know that there is no fancy blueprint for success other than the one you create for yourself based on your own experiences and education. Stay focused on your journey by doing what works for you based on where you are in your life and the direction that you are trying to go; then live by that example.

Finally, as you're ready to elevate, get a mentor. Find someone that has what you want and aspire to achieve. Find out what they did to get that thing whether spiritual, financial, business, or whatever, and do it until you can finally get it the way you want it and from there, can teach it to other people so they can teach it to other people.

That's how you build a legacy of leaders!

John Malott gets results! From humble beginnings to Founder and Chairman of *Build Your Empire*, Founder and CEO of *O'Snap Active Lifestyle*. John is a world-class entrepreneur whose superpowers lie in the areas of branding, sales, marketing, and leadership! Having served over 1 million people by way of his expert training and experiential seminars worldwide, John has the innate ability to take what appears to be complex and break it down into simple, easily executable steps. He has become one of the most sought-after business mentors, educators, and keynote speakers in the world.

He has been featured in countless global publications including *Forbes, Entrepreneur, Thrive Global, Success from Home,* and *USA TODAY.*

PREFACE

"To be a great leader is to see your position in the world as a chance to inspire others no matter what." ~ Dr. Bonita Parker

Small business owners – distinctively referred to as entrepreneurs, are a unique class of people. I mean, let's face the facts – *we just are!* You have some people who kick their heels up and wallow in the mere fantasy of what being their own boss would be like, while entrepreneurs are busy either creating their own businesses or are already knee-deep in the meat and potatoes of growing their business to the next level all the while reaping the benefits and tackling the complex path head-on.

Make no mistake that entrepreneurship is in no way a get-rich-quick scheme. Many would start their business while working for a 9 to 5 corporation and then, once they save a certain amount of money in the nest egg, or even become stabilized in their business, they will leap into full-time entrepreneurship. And it's this mentality – also known as the entrepreneurial mindset or as I like to call it, a CEO mindset – that sets them up for success. The most powerful entrepreneurs spend a large amount of time thinking and envisioning how to carry out their high goals. They are inherently creative and like being amid a new discovery and consider their mind and its ability to think outside the box to be their most valuable resource. They've always dared to dream and to make their goals come true. This imaginative quality distinguishes them from others who are afraid to dream as big or who believe themselves to be as great as they are. Those that stand out feel their originality, success, ability to create money, engage in new initiatives and do what they believe they can still imagine and achieve has no expiration date. They aren't a one-and-done kind of character.

One of the most elusive keys to success in entrepreneurship is effective leadership. While a few entrepreneurs have broken the code of transforming brilliant leadership into exceptional results, many others are still struggling.

The shifting nature of leadership just adds to the confusion. Faced with fierce competition in a global market, today's flatter, faster, more adaptable businesses require more active leadership.

The most effective businesses in training their team thoroughly examine the performance and capabilities of their current leaders and potential leaders, provide substantial development and coaching, track their progress, and then reward them. They also work to improve their leaders' self-awareness, self-management, social awareness, and social skills—what we call emotional intelligence. Let's take a closer look at what leadership looks like.

According to Webster's dictionary, the term "lead" means "to steer on a path." Furthermore, a "leader" is defined as "a person who commands authority or influence and leads others." Furthermore, "leadership" is defined as "a position as a group, organization, or institution's leader." The skill or authority to lead others."

According to the definitions above, leadership is a means of influencing a group to reach a common goal. *Wouldn't you agree?* As a result, leadership is not only about influence, but it also doesn't exist without it. The following are the leading factors that have an impact on the letters that make up the word leadership:

"LEADERSHIP"

- **L: Listen** - effective communication requires the ability to listen. Because great leaders are excellent listeners, they say less and listen more.

- **E: Enthusiasm** – demonstrated excitement and ecstatic about your goals and accomplishments.

- **A: Aspiring** - possessing high objectives and goals that you are eager to achieve more and be more.

- **D: Decisiveness** - the ability to make complex decisions and hold yourself accountable.

- **E: Empower and Encourage** - Give people more responsibility and the support they require.

- **R: Responsible** - Ability to accept responsibility for one's actions.

- **S: Supple** - aids in the development and maintenance of effective interpersonal interactions. Individuals are more likely to become friends and remain loyal to an intelligent, caring, and nice leader.

- **H: Humble -** demonstrates humility and honesty while possessing the ability to make others feel important and cherished.

- **I: Inspire with Integrity -** Encourage, motivate others by being honest and truthful.

- **P: Plan -** The ability to forecast and create alternative action steps (Plan-B) if plan-A does not go as planned.

Aside from that, there is another method to identify a person who is capable of powerful leadership. Effective leaders provide clear direction to their peers and subordinates and encourage them to commit to their roles and work together to achieve the company's goals and objectives. This also indicates that strong executives typically have a clear vision for the company and can quickly recognize the challenges and roadblocks that now stand in their way of achieving its goals. As a result, they can effectively and efficiently implement the required reforms to bring the company into the future while staying current with current business trends.

Pick up any newspaper or business publication today, such as the Financial Times, New York Times, Singapore's Straits Times, Sydney Morning Herald, or The Economist, and you'll almost certainly find an article in which a politician or an economist declares how important entrepreneurship is to the nation and that more entrepreneurs are needed to ensure economic growth and prosperity.

The goal of this book is to give insight into the growing trends of entrepreneurship and to provide perspective on the methodology of leadership and leaving your mark on the world.

Throughout the book, you'll hear from successful entrepreneurs who have paved the way for new and aspiring leaders as they shine a light on personal experiences and provide tools to aid in your growth. The appendixes house personal and business assessments from seasoned leaders to assist you in getting clear on who you are as a leader and how you show up in your greatness.

THE ROAD TO BECOMING A SUCCESSFUL ENTREPRENEUR

Having thoughts about taking the leap into entrepreneurship and starting your own business? Trust me when I say that this is probably one of the most excitingly scary things that you may ever do in your life because of the uncertainty as to whether you are leaping at the right time, in the right location, and for the right reasons.

When I first decided to step out on faith to be my own boss and leave my six-figure position in corporate America, it truly felt like heaven on earth and such an accomplishment. I remember thinking to myself as I drove away from the parking garage of my 9 to 5 saying, *"thank heavens I don't have to answer to anyone and no one can any longer dictate my worth or when I can take off from work!"* Oh, what a feeling! Not realizing that the bulk of my excitement was because I had "one-upped" my employer by resigning before they could fire me. Very little was contributory to the fact that I was embarking on something that I was wildly passionate about. BIG MISTAKE! In fact, I was scared shitless to be making such a huge move on the fly as I did.

Business, like science, has the power to combine two unconnected domains to produce something entirely new. It's not much different for individuals looking to establish their own company and be leaders in their industry. Prospective entrepreneurs should begin by exploring their interests or passions in a field, as well as the reason and goals for making such a significant shift in their lives. It is imperative that before you quit your day job, be sure that you have done extensive research and market analysis to ensure that you will indeed have a customer market and that you have something you are truly excited about starting. This kind of honesty and understanding is frequently beneficial in verifying that the justification for a proposed business is a sound one and successful leadership is imminent.

Despite the lack of research that some entrepreneurs may do, the various methods of leader development provides a positive impact for both new and aspiring leaders and their business. But leaders must first be dedicated to their own development. The effectiveness of an entrepreneur depends on their overall vision, mission, and desired goals.

Why is it so important to be effective if you want to be successful and make your mark as a leader? Because efficacy plays a crucial role in every decision-making process. It all boils down to getting the desired results to make the impact you wish to make. The most successful entrepreneurs master effectiveness because it allows them to work smarter, reducing wasted effort and time. When approached in a sloppy, haphazard, hit-or-miss manner, success is impossible to achieve. The most successful leaders don't allow ease or disorder to influence their decision-making. Before implementing any goal or strategy, they take much care to be thorough, organized, and well-prepared in an effort to stay in the flow of positive movement. Extremely effective entrepreneurial leaders inject certain habits into their daily way of living and doing business.

When I first started my journey as an entrepreneur, I had this belief that all it took was me starting a business and merely having the title of a business owner. *Crazy right!* I knew very little about the amount of work required or about how to grow my business for success and scale for sustainability. How naïve was I … but I'm 1000% positive that I was not alone in my thought process as many new entrepreneurs do go into entrepreneurship blindly and seeing only the glitz and glam of owning a business versus the grit and sacrifice needed to make it successful. One thing I realized soon enough was that there was no miracle or instant success potion that was going to make me an overnight success. Even the best ideas require endless effort, lots of patience, and plenty of know-how to achieve success. It's one thing to start a business, and a whole other beast to be successful in business and making it a part of your lifestyle. Let me shed some insight on that for you …

Being a successful entrepreneur entails much more than launching new businesses every day. It isn't about being born with specific beliefs or a certain type of mindset. *Oh no!*

Entrepreneurship is multifaceted – ever-evolving and very demanding. It's about being prepared for everything that comes your way once you step into the realm. It denotes a positive attitude toward business as well as the determination and grit required to succeed. Having a positive mind-space is the most essential habit that any future or current leader can possess. The way you think about and of yourself, your abilities, and your business plays a vital role in how you maneuver and show up on a regular basis. Don't allow emotions like fear of failure to hold a permanent residence in your mind – instead, use the thought of it as a steppingstone to push forward and take risks. Should you happen to "fail," simply assess what went wrong, learn from the mistake, and move forward.

It is no secret that roughly 20% of small businesses fail within the first year, and that number increases to 50% by the end of their fifth year (according to the Bureau of Labor Statistics). But why is this? Why are entrepreneurs failing at business at such a rapid pace?

The advantage of being an entrepreneur is that you have total control of your company and the choices you make within the company – and this includes the moves that you make for it as well. One of the primary reasons that come to mind is that many lack passion for what they are doing. They start with what I call the "kid in the candy store" syndrome where they get gleefully excited at the thought of starting a business but then grow weary once they realize the amount of work that goes into maintaining it. This brings me to a huge disadvantage of entrepreneurship. Because so much is required to grow your business, many fail to realize that entrepreneurship is like a baby that never goes to sleep and is constantly nurturing – no matter how old it gets. You wake up an entrepreneur and you go to bed an entrepreneur, and if you are not prepared, it becomes your work and your life. To be successful, entrepreneurs must possess a powerful inner drive that propels them forward so that when the going gets tough, they keep on going despite any obstacle. You see, when you put the focus on the reason you are doing it (i.e., the passion), versus what you stand to gain from it, you will win every time. *Why?* Because then, and only then, will the prospect of labor excite you enough to build up the strong desire necessary to succeed and conquer challenges, despite the numerous setbacks.

Another huge factor to consider is the lack of product or service demand. Many fail to do the research required to see if there is a need or even a market for their offering. This means doing an assessment of the market to determine the level of success you can achieve in your industry. When I started my first business as an Event Planner, I was terribly relaxed in the fact that I had a skill and was very creative. I felt that this alone was enough to carry me in business – and boy was I wrong! I did no market research to see if there was a need in the industry that I could fill; *hell, I didn't even really have a niche!* I knew that I was going to plan weddings and that was the gist of it. I did not talk to potential customers to understand what their needs or problems were, nor did I reach out to other industry professionals to assess their offering to see what they were not offering to clients so that I could fill that gap. *Mega mistake!* I only assumed that I knew what they needed and offered only that. My passion dwindled and my "career" as a wedding planner was over sooner than anticipated.

Ask! Seek! Search! Always look to learning more. Successful entrepreneurs are like sponges and seek to soak up all there is to know. They make it a practice to be curious about everything and to be open to new ideas. This curiosity keeps them asking inquiries and producing suggestions for their future actions. It is hard to deplete their creative reservoirs because they stay open and curious. They are continually pondering some modest concept that they want to pursue later. Curiosity is another factor that adds to their efficacy and success. The difference between mediocre achievement and great success is curiosity. Ordinary people stop working when they run out of creative energy. However, very successful entrepreneurs take a completely different approach in that they never stop coming up with innovative ideas or directions to take.

We can't negate the very important issue of m-o-n-e-y! This is a big fork in the road for many new entrepreneurs. And honestly speaking, *why wouldn't it be?* Despite the myth that you don't need money to start a business, it is indeed a major reason entrepreneurs maintain dual careers – a traditional 9-5 and their small business endeavor. It is also the fine line between success and failure in business. It is essential to have a financial forecast and budget in place. Equally as important is lining up your financial resources so that you can fund the necessities of keeping your business afloat – whether it's something as small as maintaining the advanced features of your website or something as major as advertising expenses. Out-of-pocket expenses can be taxing, especially if your business is not generating sufficient cash flow to cover the required expenses. This leaves very little room for financial error. Success is contingent upon figuring out how to run your business efficiently and effectively and doing so will indeed require some financial security.

The bottom line is that there are many reasons why businesses fail, but there are also just as many as to why they succeed. Making sure you are set up for success from the start is essential. Here are a few of my personal suggestions and some necessary steps to take before you take the leap.

1. Create a solid business plan before taking the leap. Think it all through and be intentional about what you want to achieve in your business. I suggest doing a 1-year plan to start. This will help to ensure you stay on track with the vision and goals that you outline for yourself. Too often new entrepreneurs forego this part of the process and end up winging it – which could prove costly in the

end. Note that the bulk of the business will fall in line for the most part when you have solid goals and objectives in place to help move your business forward.

2. Make sure your credit is up to par. There are tons of resources available to entrepreneurs to help with startup costs and expenses. *I know – I know!* Another myth is that you shouldn't start your business off with debt. That's why I would encourage you to look into grants as well to offset the amount of loan you apply for.

3. Manage your overhead costs and keep them as low as possible. Granted, every new business owner will have some startup costs and as mentioned above, some business maintenance expenses. However, if you're careful and plan accordingly, you won't fall into the trap of overextending your finances by putting out more than you're bringing in.

4. Build a list of potential supporters. Granted, the chances that your family and friends will be your primary support system are less likely, however, encourage them to share your new endeavor with their friends and colleagues. It is vital to your business that you establish a network of connections that can potentially open the door to other valuable connections to help you grow and expand your business. Another way to do this is to attend local networking events and put yourself out there to like-

minded individuals who are of mutual benefit to you. For example, if your business is event planning, you may want to connect with other planners, photographers, decorators, deejays, etc.

Another caveat to being a successful entrepreneur is to have a strong feeling of self-assurance and a positive view of your abilities and skills. What sets successful entrepreneurs apart is their assertive and powerful character. They are laser-focused and don't waste time debating the issues at hand. They are doers and action-takers. These characteristics are also what keeps them in creative mode. Successful entrepreneurs are always on the hunt for new inventions and ideas and improved methods to operate a business and enhance their products and services.

Also, a crucial characteristic of a successful entrepreneur is their willingness to adjust. When it comes to deciding on other options, they should not be obstinate. In business, the only constant is change; no one can make money in outdated ways. Evolution is the key to success, whether in terms of ideas, services, products, or technology. An entrepreneur should be willing to learn new things and keep an open mind. It is critical to recognize that the only way to stay at the top is to change and evolve with the times. This is the only way to provide better service to clients and remain competitive.

Finally, the most challenging of all – for most people who are new to entrepreneurship, is the ability to accept rejection or constructive criticism. This is an important part of being a successful business owner. Criticism reveals what or where changes are required or could be improved upon. This helps you to become more aware of company flaws so that you can be mentally equipped to correct them. As a result, embracing criticism is a fantastic approach to improvisation.

I want you to heed the following advice when building your business and establishing your success path:

➢ **Follow Your Instincts.**

Entrepreneurs have no way of knowing whether a given concept or breakthrough will succeed. If you want to be successful, trust your gut feelings and know that they will guide you in the right direction. Going with your gut also allows you to make quick decisions rather than waiting for market research results and missing out on viable opportunities.

➢ **Remain laser-focused on your goals.**

Concentrating on your objectives will allow you to see and quickly assess opportunities and filter out non-strategic activity and distractions. Superior execution — doing a terrific job of "blocking and tackling" – is the key to true entrepreneurial success. Successful entrepreneurial leaders greatly maximize their productivity by prioritizing work over socializing. For them, socializing is vital and life-giving. Once they conquer their business goals, they need to get out and about to connect with others, not just for the human interaction and emotions of closeness, but also because being in the company of others decreases stress and improves innovation. They opt to plan when they are not under any business pressures at the end of the day. This enables them to give their complete attention to those with whom they are connecting and creating relationships. They guarantee that they will perform efficiently in any location they select since they plan their life in this manner.

➢ Be Flexible and Fluid

Every entrepreneur must be adaptable, learning and adjusting to new information as it becomes available. To be a successful leader in business, you must retain an open mind and think quickly. When things go wrong, learn to pivot quickly versus getting stuck out of fear of changing gears and trying something new. As crucial as regularity is, it is imperative that leaders recognize that being able to pivot on-demand in reaction to unforeseen or changing situations is critical. Being able to change course boosts their odds of success while also improving their learning, growth, and education. The routines they follow are simple by design to be easy to sustain no matter what their circumstances are. Successful leaders make it a habit to bring the minimum necessities with them merely. This enhances productivity because they don't need anything specific to work and communicate effectively, whether at the beach or the office.

> ## Innovation

Even the most successful businesses will not maintain its position if it sits on its laurels. Stagnation caused by a lack of innovation is a death kill for a business, and the risk-reward equation significantly favors innovation. There's no doubting that innovation is moving at a breakneck pace right now, and it's pervasive in our culture. To avoid a downturn, you must have a freshness of thought that is necessary for change.

> ## Recognize Your Ecosystem

What are you doing to alleviate your consumers' pain points? Are you familiar with the other players in your industry? Who are the people that might be interested in investing in your business? Who do you go to when you need to bounce ideas around? Understanding your ecosystem has the potential to boost your company's growth trajectory significantly.

Entrepreneurship does not occur in a vacuum, and various stakeholders influence your company's life cycle. The ability to solve challenges is directly proportional to your understanding of your ecosystem.

> ## Managing Your Finances

As we mentioned above, a good entrepreneur must manage his or her finances carefully. Money is the lifeblood of any company endeavor. It is a necessary component of purchasing inventory, paying staff, marketing the company, purchasing, or repairing business equipment, and paying your salary. It needs commitment and self-control from the start to avoid making poor financial decisions or spending business funds prematurely, especially in a solo venture. Raising finances is virtually always more difficult and time-consuming than you anticipated. So, keep that in mind.

➤ **Delegation**

Stop believing you can handle everything! We entrepreneurs have a habit of having a full plate and believing that we can handle any assignment. In actuality, if we keep piling more to an already overflowing plate, it will eventually fall and be in shambles. Don't let your stubbornness (or ego ... *YEP, I said it*!) keep you from seeking assistance. Don't be hesitant to assign duties to an experienced member of your team who can execute them better or faster than you can!

➤ **A Good Support System**

Many business owners hire people that are similar to them. The key is to surround yourself with individuals who aren't like you but are excellent at what they do and what you can't. *Read that part again.* When you leave your mind open to negative outside influences, you are setting yourself up for the ultimate failure in business and as a leader. This is also why most entrepreneurs quit the journey before even getting started. When you're caught in a rut or need to talk things over, having a positive, professional network of industry veterans is by far the best move you can make. If the goal is to grow and become someone who achieves success, having an exceptionally strong and positive network to support you will aid in that process in a great way. A high-growth startup requires a strong network that can guide you and challenge you to think bigger. After all, success rises and falls on associations and surroundings; therefore, your circle of influence can be detrimental to your level of success so make sure you are giving time to the right people.

> **Get Up Early**

Effective entrepreneurs believe that the early bird who gets up early actually gets the worm. Every day begins with some physical exertion. It's how they get themselves to wake up, get their blood pounding, and their minds alert. They prefer to get to work early to minimize interruptions while they are focused on the objectives in which they set for themselves the night before. They are always generally multiple steps ahead of the game because of this. They work more effectively and with higher quality when the environment is peaceful and void of distractions. One of the best success habits that I injected into my life was to map out my goals daily – prioritizing and only focusing on those which needed to get done that day. This keeps me feeling inspired and accomplished as I can clear the list by the end of my workday.

➢ **Get Proper Rest**

Successful entrepreneurs seldom underestimate the importance of sleep. They want to be sharp, emotionally available, and on the ball in all aspects of their lives. The bi-directional relationship between sleep and stress has been demonstrated and extensively documented: a lack of sleep causes an increase in emotional reactivity and a decrease in frustration tolerance, both of which contribute to another night of bad sleep. It's a vicious circle. Successful entrepreneurs do not want to spend their nights worrying about how ineffectively or poorly they handled circumstances or people during the day. Effectiveness becomes impossible if poor sleeping patterns are not addressed. Successful entrepreneurs believe that work will continue to exist. They carve out the time for sleep that they require and benefit as a result. They are less likely to have emotions of burnout, lost productivity, increased health difficulties, and missed days of work because they value their sleep and make sure they receive enough of it. No matter what ... *do not* get caught up in the theory that "successful people don't sleep" – which is usually said to new entrepreneurs as a "dig" at their level of commitment to their goals and business.

➢ **Be Concise**

Effective business leaders swear by simplicity as their hidden weapon. They're known for creating and following simple yet functional rituals almost religiously. Creating simple procedures allows them to avoid taking on demands that are beyond their capacity. When they aren't stressed, successful entrepreneurs are the most effective in attaining their goals. As a result, they impose boundaries on themselves and are more concerned with delivering high-quality work than with pleasing others. They gain a sense of agency over their lives, their workload, and their ability to operate as effectively and efficiently as possible because of the restrictions they set for themselves.

> ➤ **Keep a Journal**

Making it a habit to write in a journal is one of the simplest strategies to improve performance. Successful entrepreneurs sit down in peace to write down their deepest thoughts and feelings – whether business-related or personal. They make to-do lists, set goals, or write to vent their frustrations. Writing has been shown to offer several advantages. It necessitates participation from both sides of the brain, resulting in a more full and imaginative brainstorming or problem-solving process. Writing is also important for calming down emotional reactivity. It relieves stress and conflict-related emotions by providing a much-needed break from the daily grind of constant chatting, emailing, accepting calls, and other distractions that come with technological devices alone. Finally, writing is important to highly effective entrepreneurs because it connects them to the more existential aspects of life, reminding them of the wider picture of what they're doing.

➢ **Make No Excuses**

Successful entrepreneurs are not excuse-makers. They take accountability for their actions (or lack thereof) and the outcomes of those actions. They are forthright about their "why" and can openly admit to their shortcomings. The truth is that no one is perfect, nor is anyone exempt from coming face-to-face with obstacles. Making excuses can become very easy when you aren't apt to ownership and accountability.

CONQUERING THE INVISIBLE ENEMIES

Obviously, many qualities and attributes are required to thrive in business. So, does this imply that to succeed in business, an entrepreneur must be a superhero?

Certainly not. Only a few people are born with all the wonderful abilities they need to achieve success in life. Successful business owners, on the other hand, appear to work around their shortcomings by learning as they go, admitting their flaws, and bolstering their weaknesses - a process that appears to help them overcome their concerns and face the invisible enemies that often paralyze them.

Fear is a prevalent feeling that is frequently expressed through excuses, delay, or inaction. Fear, according to many psychologists, lies at the foundation of most human issues. Four of the most prevalent worries linked with starting a business are listed here.

1. Your age.

What age is considered too old or too young to operate a business? My first business started as a hobby. I was 26 years old and took on the task of planning my big sister's wedding. I had truly no clue what I was doing because prior to that, I had only planned small social gatherings and birthday parties. But I figured – what the hell!

You plan one event, you've planned them all, right? While it was a huge success and I received a few requests to plan other weddings afterwards, the thought of starting a business at almost 30 years old terrified me. I was under the assumption that successful people started as children. I mean, look at Michael Jackson who started as a child with his brothers as the Jackson 5. That's the ideal that I had in my mind, not realizing that you had someone like Colonel Sanders, who at age 64, invented Kentucky Fried Chicken and began selling his secret recipe to franchisees. There was also Ray Kroc, an Illinois malt shake machine salesperson, at 52 years old, he bought four California hamburger shops and retooled them into the McDonald's empire. And so, according to some industry experts, the number of entrepreneurs over the age of 50 is expected to rise dramatically.

At the other end of the scale, Michael Dell, the founder of Dell Computer, began his first business at the age of 13. His computer parts business, which he ran out of his college dorm room, was bringing in $80,000 per month by the time he was 19. Bill Gates, not to be outdone, founded Microsoft at the youthful age of 19. Millennials are also launching enterprises at nearly twice the rate of their elders. The general message is that age is not a determining factor in sustaining a business. The importance of attitude, courage, and action is significantly greater. *So, no matter what age you are, start that darn business!*

2. A lack of funds.

There's no denying that having a large sum of money or a nice-sized nest egg in the bank makes launching a business easier. However, a sizable proportion of successful entrepreneurs are adamant that possessing more than average startup capital has little bearing on overall performance. In fact, many hard-nosed entrepreneurs argue that starting a business with as little money as possible is advantageous. *Yep! You heard me correctly.*

The belief is that when given a considerable sum of money, too many people waste it on things they don't need, such as an office, a secretary, or expensive computer equipment. Whereas having a modest amount of initial funds, on the other hand, emphasizes frugality and efficiency. If you don't believe me, consider the hundreds of thousands of people worldwide who started their businesses with little more than a few dollars and a burning passion for seeing their idea succeed. Disney, Apple, Hewlett Packard, and the Mattel toy company, for example, all started in garages. Jim Casey, as a youngster from Seattle, created UPS with $100, two bicycles, one phone, and six employees. And we can't fail to mention the many successful rappers and entertainers who had one mixtape, made hundreds of copies of it just to sell out of the trunk of their cars.

Remember Hallmark? Joyce C. Hall, just eighteen years old, founded the Hallmark greeting card company with an armful of postcards she held in two shoeboxes. In 1964, Phil Knight and Bill

Bowerman each put $300 into a consignment of athletic shoes and sold them out of the trunk of their car during track races. And what do you think happened there? *Nike baby!* Thomas Monaghan, who spent his childhood in and out of orphanages and foster homes (and was kicked out of everything from a Catholic seminary to the Marine Corps as a result), founded Domino's Pizza by transforming a bankrupt pizza parlor - half of which he traded for his Volkswagen Beetle - into the United States' leading pizza delivery service.

Simply put, business success is frequently dependent on 10% capital and 90% guts (as the old adage goes). To put it another way, *those who can't earn money without it are unlikely to make money with it.*

Mindpower, diligence, and passion are significantly more influential.

3.   The Fear of Being Rejected.

Whew! This is one that many entrepreneurs allow to keep them leaping. That ole question of *"what if no one wants what I have?"* or *"what if no one supports me?"* My response to that is "ok, so what if they don't. Then what?" Rejection or as I personally like to refer to it – *elective timing* – is a part of life, not just business. But since we are on that topic, let's stay here.

As a bestselling author and publisher, not a day goes by where I don't wonder whether people will purchase my books or support my business. But I'm reminded that people will buy, invest, and support at the exact moment that they feel compelled to do so. *It's really that simple.* You can have the best product on the market and a potential customer may not purchase it from you at the launch date; but if you market the same product six months later, they may buy at that time. That's why it's called elective timing. They didn't say no to the product. They said no to supporting it *at that time.*

Most successful business owners would easily confess that rejection is a part of the journey to success. *And here's why they triumph in the end ...* they continuously put in the effort rather than giving up at the baseline. *But I didn't tell you anything that I'm 100% certain you did not already know, right?*

Successful business entrepreneurs learn to deal with rejection, failure, and hardship and then push forward. Let's take King C. Gillette, the inventor of the safety razor, who was humiliated for six years by companies, financiers, and toolmakers who laughed aloud at his brilliant new device. When King finally decided to produce his innovation, sales skyrocketed by 1,000 percent every year! He got his "no's" handed to him – and even got laughed at for his brilliant idea. The number of yeses that he got, in turn, afforded him massive wealth and the ability to become a sustainable household name in the retail industry for many years to come – all because he kept going.

Such comeback stories are the motivational push that new entrepreneurs and business leaders need to hear about. Indeed, millennials are more likely than their elders to learn from their mistakes, brush them aside, and then use them to their advantage. The takeaway here is that winning is often a mental game. Success is frequently nothing more than failure turned inside out for those who have the resilience to stay in the game.

4. Inadequate training or experience.

Evidence demonstrates that a college diploma does not guarantee success. Indeed, it can appear that way at times, but I'm here to confirm that that is not the case. Many entrepreneurial endeavors barely require more than a high school diploma. You have so many industry business leaders who did not go beyond that point. After dropping out of college, Steve Jobs and Stephen Wozniak started Apple Computer. Neither of them had any prior business experience. Michael Dell, the multibillionaire founder of Dell Computer, is a college dropout as well. John Bond, the former chairperson of HSBC (one of the world's largest banks), never attended college. *Still not convinced?* Consider the case of Ian Leopold, a college student who his professor dismissed due to an unrealistic business plan he submitted in class. With the same method, Leopold turned a $48 investment into $4 million in ten years by following his intuition (writing university guidebooks). And finally, there's Anita Roddick, the founder of The Body Shop, who advised entrepreneurs to "stay away from business schools" in the final years of her life. She believed that business schools place an excessive emphasis on the financial side of the business while neglecting the crucial human element.

Of course, this does *not* negate the need for education and experience in starting and running a successful business. A mentor told me several years ago, "it's never about how much you know, it's about applying the knowledge you do have and tweaking it as you go." His point is that not knowing everything there is to know about running a business is not bad. The only shame comes from refusing to recognize it and rejecting the need to improve. I learned the majority of what I know hands-on through trial and error. I achieved success very early in my career. Granted, it wasn't until later – much later in life that I decided to go back to school to get credentialed and expand my knowledge into other areas of my business niche.

The core message here is to not be discouraged by not having prefixes, suffixes, and other initials attached to your name before getting started on your success journey. There are many online courses, mentors, support platforms, and resources that can teach you what you need or show you what you're missing to elevate.

EXCLUSIVE INTERVIEW WITH BUSINESS COACH & TV PERSONALITY, BERSHAN SHAW

Thank you Bershan for agreeing to contribute to this project. As a leader who has achieved great success through hard work and dedication, I have witnessed you grow and attack entrepreneurship with fearlessness and such grace.

What was the pivotal moment that made you decide to leap into entrepreneurship?

I knew I wanted more. I was young making money for someone else. I was bartending trying to make ends meet while pursuing my dreams as a writer, actor, and motivational speaker. I knew I was good with people. While bartending, I realized I was bringing in $12,000 to $15,000 by myself on average. I was the superstar bartender that everyone came to visit. I took control of my position and I started booking guests, companies, and more, and then one day I woke up and said, *"Why am I making so much money for someone else, I can be making the money for myself."* That's when the lightbulb went off and decided to open my own restaurant/bar, and to my surprise, one of my favorites clients told me that he would support me by investing in the endeavor - and he did. It was December 18, 2006, when I realized that I needed to step into my big girl pants and make my own money. I was blessed to have someone who supported my vision just as much as I believed in it. Sometimes all it takes is just one person to see the passion and belief in yourself that you possess to support you.

What was your biggest lesson learned along the way and how did it shape your path going forward?

My biggest lesson learned was to NEVER EVER GIVE UP. I know it sounds cliche and I know we have heard it before but the top one-percenters that you see achieving success have all made a decision, stayed focused, and never gave up on that thing that they wanted to achieve. I know it can get scary and I know things may not seem like it's going well but that's the test – to either quit or keep going. I'm a fighter. I'm a warrior. I always choose to keep going.

How do you define success?

Success is when you are living your dream. When you are living your passion. When you would do your dream job and not get paid for it. Money can come but you can still feel empty inside. Success is the feeling of being complete. That you have learned, grown, and are where you want to be. The journey never ends ... you just keep learning and growing. That's success.

What are your core success habits and principles?

My routine is simple. Once I decided that I was going to pursue entrepreneurship with everything in me, I had to look at what the real leaders and successful people were doing. They all had a schedule or ritual that they followed every single day and adopted as a way of life. I did the same. I start by getting up early daily at 5 am – meditating and fueling my soul with affirmations of positivity or reading something positive. Another thing that I do is journal – every single day before I set my goal intentions. This helps me avoid burnout and most importantly, it prevents any negative energy from infiltrating my mind. It's a must! I stay focused on those goals and minimize my time on social media – I only spend 30 minutes max on social media.

I highly encourage all entrepreneurs to adopt a daily routine that works for them to help them stay balanced and focused. It's so easy to get off track otherwise.

What are three common myths about entrepreneurship that you most often hear? Please elaborate.

The most common myths that I hear from new entrepreneurs – and even those who are not in business but harbor a fear of stepping out in their passion, all say that entrepreneurship is too hard. Granted, it's not the easiest thing in the world to do, but with success – comes dedication and consistency. As long as you have those things, you can make it.

Another myth is that you can't make money. Tell that to the many successful business leaders out here who invented, created, and steadfastly went out on a limb and took a leap. Bill Gates, Elon Musk, Steve Jobs and so many others – had an idea and made billions from it. That sounds like money to me!

Another dispelling myth is that you can't find good help. Listen, these are all excuses and reasons to not get started. If you make a decision, stay focused on it, and take massive action to accomplish your dreams and goals. The sky is the limit!

Bershan Shaw didn't earn the nickname "The Warrior Coach" by accident. Her career as a sought-after international motivational speaker, business coach, women's advocate, and author was forged through her dedication, perseverance, and a brush with death.

As a two-time breast cancer survivor with a three-month prognosis, Bershan summoned her inner warrior to conquer the impossible, defy the odds, and beat her illness. Now, she uses her leadership skills to bring a no-nonsense approach to motivate others, Bershan founded Warrior Training International to help individuals reach their full potential.

Bershan is an industry pioneer in transformational coaching, executive leadership training, and diversity and inclusion implementation. Along with these, she also coaches execs in technology, consumer products, emotional intelligence, and unconscious bias. Her unique background, dynamic presenting style, humor, real-world techniques, and practical strategies leave every audience, from Amazon to the Essence Music Festival to UBS and Johns Hopkins University feeling energized, transformed, and ready to take on new challenges. Her media appearances include features on NBC, ABC, Fox, and OWN.

To learn more about Bershan Shaw, please visit www.bershan.com

32

"

From the biggest challenge in your life will come your biggest opportunity. Don't run away from failures and mistakes, grow from them.

~ Bershan Shaw

34

FACING THE UGLY TRUTH ABOUT ENTREPRENEURSHIP

Many myths accompany entrepreneurship. I'm personally inclined to believe that many stem from things that were embedded in our minds as a youth, from either our parents, grandparents or other people of influence. Think about it. How many times have you heard your parents or grandparents say, *"When you finish school, you get a good job so you can pay your bills."* Or maybe this one, *"If you're not going to college, you need to get out there and get a job."* You will rarely never hear a push for entrepreneurship. That could have very well been a sign of the times. Today, entrepreneurship is certainly more prevalent and lucrative – if you can ignore the mythical chatter long enough to pursue the level of success you desire.

I heard it all when I first took the leap and I will admit that it was a little scary to step away from the comforts of a guaranteed paycheck every two weeks to grinding to ensure that I made enough to cover my monthly bills and keep me afloat. Of course, fear isn't the only invisible enemy that keeps entrepreneurs from succeeding. Numerous fallacies also obstruct the initial critical procedures. Here are my eight most notable entrepreneurship misunderstandings.

1. **Starting a business is easy and simple.**

It's difficult to understand why anyone would think this, especially given the fact that many people who start a business fail. Only one-third of successful entrepreneurs in the United States can claim to have a positive cash flow higher than their pay and costs for more than three months seven years after starting their business.

2. **A large sum of money is required to fund a startup.**

There are many who started with zero to hundreds of dollars. Contrary to popular belief, a typical startup in the United States does not require tens of thousands of dollars to get started. How can you start a business with such a minimal amount of money? Entrepreneurs who succeed do everything they can to keep prices down. Instead of purchasing equipment, they borrow it. They prefer to rent rather than buy. They also shift fixed costs into variable costs by providing commissions instead of salaries to their staff, or even better, they will outsource to freelancers. There are so many ways to keep costs to a reduced level due to the number of resources available to entrepreneurs nowadays.

3. **Venture capitalists are a good source of funding for new businesses.**

Unless the company is in the computer or biotech industries, that is. In the United States, venture capitalists invest over 3,000 companies per year (one-third of which are in the initial stages of development), with computer hardware (and software), semiconductors, communication, and biotechnology accounting for roughly 81 percent of all venture capital dollars. In fact, the chances of a startup receiving funding from a venture capitalist are one in 4,000. (Which is worse than the odds of dying from a fall while taking a shower).

4. You are born an entrepreneur.

I can't tell you how many times I've heard this in my 15-year tenure as an entrepreneurial leader. It's almost laughable in a sense as it paints a picture that only a few possess what it takes to be in this space, when in fact, just about anyone can be an entrepreneur if they apply themselves and learn the tricks of their preferred trade. Now, some people may catch on or adjust to it faster than others but there are no hard facts that support this theory.

5. There is a "secret sauce" to success.

Some leaders won't tell you this, but there is really *NO* secret sauce to achieving success. I know you are in shock. It's easy to look at what others are doing or have done and think that it is a simple process. You have no idea what that person went through to get to that point, or how many times they have tried and failed miserably before finally getting it right. I can almost guarantee that the only "secrets" they used were applied knowledge, consistency, dedication, and a strong support system. No one that I know of has ever gotten to the top without the help of someone else – coupled with the aforementioned.

6. Banks will not give money to startup businesses.

According to Federal Reserve data, banks account for 16 percent of all financing granted to businesses that are two years old or younger. This is 3% more than the next greatest source, trade creditors, and a smidgeon more than the most popular capital sources: friends, family, business angels, venture capitalists, strategic investors, and government agencies. However, I would caution against taking out a big loan in the first year of starting your business (unless it's a franchise or another business with a built-in blueprint) as you will use this time to really bring life to your idea and iron out the kinks. Once you have a clear concise business plan in place to see how you will properly allocate the funds to make your business profitable, I would wait until that point to seek outside funding sources and eliminate the risk of repayment before your business is profitable.

7. Entrepreneurship is the ultimate freedom.

Unfortunately, while this does sound good, it is not the case at all. Granted you will feel a high sense of relief from transitioning from a traditional 9-5 – and this could very well just be due to the curb appeal of not working for someone else. However, what people fail to mention is that most often than not, you are trading the old demands for new and bigger sacrifices as unlike with a traditional job, there is no closing bell for when you can stop working.

8. Having your own business guarantees wealth.

Listen! And listen good ... you will be lucky if you can turn a profit by year two or even break even within your first five years. Starting your business is not a surefire way to millionaire status. Don't get me wrong, there are a select few that will get it right the first go-around, but not everyone. However, time, consistency, and dedication will eventually pay off in your favor.

GETTING RID OF NEGATIVITY

Perhaps it's clear why so many people opt to work for someone else rather than establish their own business. Simply said, starting a business is difficult, and the odds of success are slim. However, if establishing a business seems out of reach because the people around you - rather than the facts - are filling your head with negative beliefs, the following advice from seasoned business professionals may be worth considering:

- Generally speaking, most people will tell you what you can't do rather than what you can.
- It doesn't imply you can't succeed just because someone doesn't believe in you.
- Without your permission, no one can make you feel lesser.
- Your past doesn't need to taint your future.
- It doesn't matter where you came from; what matters is where you're going.

- You'll have a lot better chance of success if you concentrate on what you desire rather than what others deny you.
- Once the fear of the unknown (and the known) is acknowledged, it can be managed.

CREATING A POSITIVE SUCCESS DEFINITION

Still hesitant to take a chance and venture into the unknown? You're not the only one who feels this way. Even seasoned entrepreneurs are prone to comparing themselves to unrealistic standards and seeing where they fall short through the lens of other people. For example, a good friend who's also an entrepreneur once told me that she didn't believe that she was good enough to be a speaker. This was odd because there was no doubt in my (or anybody else's) mind that she was set up to be one of the most sought-after speakers.

'How long have you been speaking?' I inquired.

She said, 'Five years.'

'How many women do you know that has made it to the point where you are now?'

She replied, 'Not too many that I know of.'

'So why are you focusing on where they are – when you are further along?'

She said, 'I know. I'm just questioning whether I have what it takes to go further. How do you know when you've made it?'

I responded, 'This industry is ever-evolving and with every step forward, there's another mountain to climb. You keep climbing until your knees give out – but by then, you'll have already built a legacy of speakers who would be more than happy – even honored – to continue the climb for you. That's when you know you've made it.'

She understood what I was saying. She was conflating her drive to improve with her fear of failing. Like so many others, she saw other entrepreneurs with more things than she did and believed she was missing out on something rather than trusting the path that she was on as being the right way to go. *What is the message?* Keep your expectations in check and learn to see your ambitions as a staircase rather than a one-time shot to the moon. This does not imply settling for less; rather, it implies being practical and forward-thinking in your goals. *"The worry and insecurities of running a business never ends,"* someone once told me. Indeed, overcoming the daily nagging fear that even after servicing a satisfied customer or delivering a great keynote, we are effectively unemployed until the next consumer can be found. This is central to the concept of entrepreneurship. It's just something we must get used to as entrepreneurs.

Starting a business is an eclectic, all-or-nothing undertaking full of misconceptions, paradoxes, delight, defeats, and advice, as you can see (both wanted and unwanted). With that in mind, the wisdom of entrepreneurs has been completed (as has every chapter), and as a word of advice, don't forget to take notice of the following summary:

- Know that you can't change what you tolerate in business or life.
- Be truthful about what you want and need.
- Accept the fact that some things in life can only be learned, not taught.
- Keep in mind that fear is a gift. It's the natural way for nature to keep you awake.
- Consider the acronym for fear: False Evidence Appearing Real.
- Make a list of the things you're frightened of (it's not that scary now, is it?).
- Find out if anyone else has faced similar worries and how they overcame them.
- Rip up the list you made earlier.
- Know that if there are unresolved questions, there is no trust or safety.
- Write down what must be done to map out the path you want to take.

- Begin your journey toward your goal by obtaining as much relevant information as possible.

- Tailoring it to your target consumers, location, and business type you want to start. By educating yourself, you have nothing to lose.

- Every day is a crisis for an entrepreneur (according to Philip Knight, founder of Nike)

BUSINESS SUCCESS SECRETS *REVEALED!*

There are so many principal factors that go into running a successful business. While different entrepreneurs assess success in diverse ways, certain techniques of reaching success should be part of your business process if you want it to flourish.

COMPONENTS OF A SUCCESSFUL BUSINESS

1. Planning

This is the most crucial and first part of any business. Business planning will determine whether your entrepreneurial venture succeeds or fails because it contains your company's makeup, goals and objectives, growth estimates, product releases, marketing tactics, and revenue generation.

An effective business plan can direct your company's entire trajectory down the road maps to becoming the success you've always envisioned. Defining your company's vision, mission, and goals is the first step in planning. It will be easier to keep your company focused on the activities that generate sales and profit once you have developed a sound business strategy.

2. Financial Management

Without effective financial management, it will be difficult, if not impossible, for a business to progress and become successful. Only by properly crunching the data can you achieve long-term and profitable growth. This refers to your capacity to correctly track and assess your company's financial and non-financial drivers. This makes creating and managing your business budget a breeze.

Simultaneously, a thorough awareness of business expenses will simplify you to run your company within budgetary constraints. If you can't keep track of your business spending, you'll quickly get into debt, disappoint your investors, and risk the failure of your company. To summarize, every sensible businessperson recognizes the importance of financial management in business, which is why most entrepreneurs would rather delegate the financial aspects of their operations to someone more qualified in that field.

3. Marketing

Your company's driving force is marketing. Your company will not reach its sales, profit, or growth projections if proper and effective marketing tactics are not in place. In fact, a lack of good marketing is the most common reason for a company's demise.

True success is achieved when your company is always in the minds of the people who matter, resulting in a consistent flow of leads and people down the conversion funnel.

Everyone in the organization must be involved for your marketing to be effective. Every employee at every level, including those who are not part of the marketing team, must work together to attract the kind of individuals for whom your company delivers goods and services.

4. Employee Retention.

One of the most crucial and undervalued components of running a successful business is building and retaining a team. Unfortunately, because they have forgotten the adage that it takes a village to make a dream come true, new business owners are unwilling to invest in human capital development.

You must be willing to hire the proper people and educate them on the mechanisms that make your business run for it to succeed. In addition, you should be eager to seek out talent and empower them to help your company achieve its goals.

It's crucial to remember that hiring top personnel is only one part of running a successful business. It's also critical that you set up a method to keep them safe. One of the elements that keep employees in a company is financial compensation. However, employees also think about the work atmosphere, professional advancement, and, most importantly, benefits packages. When your employees understand that they are covered in the event of a workplace injury or disability, they will not only stay but also work more efficiently.

5. Relationship management and customer service

Customers are the lifeblood of any business, and they play a critical part in its success or failure. You won't be able to create sales, profit, or reach your growth plans if your company doesn't have clients.

However, simply having consumers is insufficient to ensure corporate success. If you have dissatisfied customers, you're only a few steps away from having no customers. Therefore, maintaining a positive customer relationship is critical in any organization.

It is your responsibility as a business owner and your workers to keep your consumers happy and content, and you must think of innovative ways to accomplish it. Providing only high-quality goods and services is one of the quickest ways to ensure customer happiness. Another option is always to be willing to listen and positively engage with customers.

If you can provide excellent customer service, you will discover that your marketing and publicity costs will decrease due to word-of-mouth advertising from your consumers.

EXCLUSIVE INTERVIEW WITH PROFIT COACH & SUCCESS MOGUL, SUSIE CARDER

I had the sheer honor of meeting Susie in 2016 when I made the radical decision to plant feet on her campus in California to be a part of her Global Leadership program that she spearheaded alongside industry leader, Lisa Nichols. Susie, your personality was infectious and your mindset was absolutely brilliant, to say the least. It is an honor and privilege to have you share your wisdom on this project. You have certainly made your mark!

What was the pivotal moment that made you decide to leap into entrepreneurship?

The vocation I chose made me an entrepreneur! I didn't realize that's what I was choosing at the time but I learned very quickly!

I was a hairdresser, and I found myself a single mom with two little girls and no child support or alimony so I had a wake-up call. *If it was meant to be it was up to me.* I put everything I had into building one of the top salons in the country – we were the top 1% in the nation and the top 10% in the world. We earned that by the dollars we produced and the level of productivity we poured out consistently. From there, I went on to build the largest training organization in the industry, old that for millions to Milady.

In my tenure as an entrepreneur, I'm humbled and proud to say that I've been blessed to have built ten organizations – two of which are 10-million-dollar companies! I this process, I've learned that I am not an employee. I absolutely love creating and building organizations!

What was your biggest lesson learned along the way and how did it shape your path going forward?

There have been so many lessons, it's hard to pick the biggest one. Each one has left an impact. I would have to say that building a company from the ground up and selling it for millions without a formal (traditional) education. I am a rouge entrepreneur who invested in learning everything I needed to know in business on my own. I took an employment law class and learned what to do differently so that I could represent myself in the event I ever got sued. If I needed to understand finances, I took a small business finance class. If I wanted to be an effective manager, I took communication courses and leadership training. I watch entrepreneurs today and what I see is that they are waiting for it to work out vs. making it happen. Business is a journey and a challenge. Business is designed to cause breakdowns, the bigger you play, the bigger the breakdown so you must be willing to get comfortable with breakdown. We are always learning how to do it differently more effectively.

If you had to give an aspiring entrepreneur a "starting point," where would that point be and why?

PLEASE put your business plan together! You will have a 70% more success rate when you get your plan in place! Spend the time upfront thinking about what you will do and how you will go about making it happen! This will save you hundreds of thousands of dollars if you spend the time to do it right. *If you fail to plan, you plan to fail.* Simple as that!

What are your core success habits and principles?

I live by my core values which are always *faith* first, *family* second, and *career* third. This helps me keep in perspective why I am working so hard.

The second success habit is everything, and I mean everything is in my schedule. If it's not in the schedule, it's not getting done. By using this as a solid structure, it allows me to accomplish more. It allows me to say "no" because my schedule dictates my availability.

The third thing I do is pay myself a paycheck. I am in the budget just like any other staff member and I pay myself a proper paycheck. Statistically speaking, 88% of small businesses make less than 100K a year in gross sales. Only 1.5% reach a million in sales. I plan everything out so that I can pay myself an amazing salary and live an abundant life!

What – in your opinion – is the difference between passion and purpose and how do they correlate to becoming a great leader/leadership?

First, if you're not passionate about what you are doing as your business, either quit or sell it and find something else. Your passion will fuel your purpose and your excitement for what you do. I help entrepreneurs make it to the million-dollar club! I want to play a big game and help clients achieve that. I love, love, love what I do and it doesn't ever feel like I am working. I believe I am doing my God-given assignment. I believe that your gift from God is your life and your gift back to God is what you do with your life! Figure out that thing that you are so great at that you will do it for FREE and monetize it so you'll never work again.

Nowadays leadership is learned and can be trained on; passion and purpose are more about what you are born to do. Did you know that 76% of people in jobs hate to go to work? That is so sad to me. Life is too short to hate what you do! When you love what you do, you want to figure out how to do more and how to find the right people to help you do more. As leaders, we need to find someone who can coach us and hold us accountable for being great leaders. Too many times I have worked with entrepreneurs who allowed their egos to get in the way and they become horrible leaders because they forgot what the bigger purpose was or is with their team. Your passion and purpose with a great coach you can develop your leadership.

What motivates you to keep pushing forward?

What motivates me is my family! They are my WHY! I wanted to give my children a different life than I had. I grew up in an abusive home; we experienced horrible things as children; we were poor, broke, and broken. I made a decision early on that my life would be different – now it hasn't been perfect, but I can say that I have created a life that is unrecognizable because I am a successful entrepreneur and leader in my industry.

Also, helping my clients achieve success keeps me going. The excitement I feel by helping others create their wealth is unlike anything else! *It's Amazing!*

SUSIE CARDER, *PROFIT COACH | SUCCESS MOGUL*

Susie Carder started as a low-paid hairdresser trying to support her two little girls. But working for someone else became a challenge (to say the least). So, she decided to do whatever it took to create her own business.

After much blood, sweat, and tears (mixed with cheap mascara), she went on to create, not one, but two $10 Million companies!

Her core genius is the ability to simplify complicated issues by creating simple, proven systems that are guaranteed to create dramatic growth for any company. She has helped over 100,000 entrepreneurs increase their revenues by more than 3000%, create radical business strategies, and ramp up from ordinary to explosive. She has worked with top business moguls including John Assaraf, Lisa Nichols, Steve Harvey, Doug Carter, and Paul Mitchell.

Her newest book, *Power Your Profit*, is a bulletproof start-to-finish plan for taking your business from startup mode to the multi-million-dollar mark.

To learn more and connect with Susie, please visit her website: www.susiecarder.com

"

*If you fail to plan, you plan
to fail. Simple as that!*

~ Susie Carder

THE IMPORTANCE OF BUILDING A LEGACY OF LEADERS

Entrepreneurial leadership entails organizing and encouraging a group of people to work toward a common goal through innovation, risk management, seizing opportunities, and managing a dynamic organizational environment. I'd like to think of being a great leader as the ability to leave a lasting footprint on the lives of others and build (or breed) other leaders who can carry out your vision after you're gone. A legacy of leaders if you will.

Do you have what it takes to be a great leader? Have you taken the time to map out what your leadership legacy looks like? Ambitious entrepreneurs have a fervent desire to leave their mark behind. Therefore, it is certainly worth it to map out how you want this to look in terms of your overall contribution to your industry, your business, and those you inspire. How do you do this?

It is well understood that leadership looks differently to different people based on their own understanding of what it means to be a leader – and thus what it takes to become a *great* one. So, identifying what that means to you is the first step of the process. There is no cookie-cutter definition for leadership as it can encompass many distinct aspects. You can be a leader by invention, a leader by revenue/wealth generation, a leader by education, or perhaps you prefer being a leader by the corporate organization. You may have a great concept for a new product or service and even a sound business plan to back it up, but if you want your business to succeed in the long run, you'll need to have the leadership characteristics to turn your vision into a lifelong reality.

There are a plethora of responsibilities that accompany leadership. The best leaders inspire others, serve as role models, and represent their business in a positive manner. To be a leader, you don't necessarily need employees, however, having individuals with whom you have built a relationship – such as clients, customers, mentees, and even mentors – is vital. How successful you are at inspiring others boils down to one key factor – how well you engage others and the level at which you interact with them. Keep in mind that just because you are in a leadership position, doesn't mean that you do not need a trusted source to bounce ideas off or even seek guidance and assistance from in times when you need it. In order for people to want to stand behind your vision and mission, it would behoove you to paint a picture so vividly exciting that others have no choice but to stand behind you and support it. Good leaders have the tendency and ability to put any ego they have to the side to seek and accept constructive feedback. This is also a very good way to build on the relationships to ensure that you have properly aligned with advocates who will support and help carry out your legacy. This is where *asking* overpowers the need to *dictate.*

SUCCESS PRINCIPLES OF A GREAT LEADER IN ENTREPRENEURSHIP

Have you heard of the phrase, "lead by example"? *Of course, you have!* When I think about what that means, I am instantaneously drawn to the notion that when leaving your mark – your legacy – it's more about how well you conduct yourself as a leader versus the accomplishments and/or vision that you leave behind. You want to make sure that your actions are indicative of the desired output that you are setting out to accomplish because who you are as a person, sets the tone for who you will be as a leader.

A successful leader will constantly have one if not both, eyes focused on the future. They think several steps ahead on every difficulty and are always on the lookout for fresh growth prospects. This future-oriented mindset is beneficial for a variety of reasons. For starters, it reduces the desire for rapid gratification—rather than pursuing the simpler or shorter path; these entrepreneurs are willing to make compromises in exchange for a more promising long-term future. They're also more likely to use long-term solutions to problems rather than patchwork solutions, which are frequently unstable and unsustainable. For example, Amazon CEO Jeff Bezos is known for reinvesting in his company on a regular basis, forsaking short-term profitability in favor of long-term growth opportunities. Remember, success isn't about instant gratification, it's also not a race. Success is a marathon to the finish line – you must not only prepare strategically but mentally as well. Let's look at some of the mental characteristics of becoming a successful leader in business.

> ### Self-Confidence

Good leaders exude self-assurance. Self-assured people captivate others and convey a sense of assurance. Clients, customers, and joint ventures will all benefit from your confidence. You'll find it easier to persuade investors that you're worth the money. Furthermore, there is actual research that suggests self-assured people are better entrepreneurs. According to a study published in the journal Applied Psychology, successful entrepreneurs had much higher confidence levels than entrepreneurial students and students who were not interested in business.

> ### Communication Capabilities

If you ask any successful leader to name the top ten concepts that helped them achieve, chances are they'll say communication. Communication is the "most critical quality any leader can possess," according to billionaire Richard Branson. Communication is a crucial skill because it can improve all your other abilities. To create sales, rally the team, handle disputes, negotiate transactions, recover from PR catastrophes, and make pitches to the media or investors, you'll need communication abilities.

Speaking, knowing your audience, and carefully selecting your words can help you avoid miscommunications, saving you time and money.

> **Self-Care**

While most of these characteristics are concerned with how entrepreneurs interact with their surroundings, it's also crucial to highlight how successful leaders care for themselves. For example, if you get insomnia and make poor dietary choices, your productivity will suffer, and you will not lead effectively. The most successful entrepreneurs recognize that their physical and mental well-being are critical to their success. They're willing to put in a few more hours each day to get enough sleep, consume healthy foods, exercise, and learn new things.

A morning routine is used by many successful entrepreneurs to feel centered and to get into the correct mentality for the day.

> **Adaptability**

Some of the world's most successful startups could only succeed because their founders were willing to pivot. For example, it may be difficult to imagine now, but YouTube began as a dating site. It would not have become the household name it is now if it had only focused on dating services, but it adapted and succeeded.

Unexpected developments and market changes might jeopardize your chances of success, no matter how well you research your business idea or how confident you are that it will succeed. You must be prepared to adapt on the go, which may need major changes to your business plan. You may not be able to survive if you cling too strongly to outdated ideals. This could be accomplished by employing adaptive leadership ideas in the workplace.

> ### Risk-taking that is calculated

Successful leadership requires the ability to assess risks and the bravery to take calculated risks comfortably with the probabilities of success. Because starting a business involves a great deal of risk, you must have a natural tolerance for it. That can be a good thing if it's managed well because it allows you to do things that more "safer" entrepreneurs won't. This can make you stand out, and if the risk pays off, you'll be in a stronger position to succeed than most. Of course, this does not imply that you should be willy-nilly with your actions; be smart, think it through, and then leap without fear!

> ### Continuous Learning and Education

Bill Gates and Steve Jobs are well-known for dropping out of college to create their companies, but that doesn't mean they stopped learning. While many of history's greatest leaders in business and other industries have received a formal education, there are also informal methods that work as well. Learning is not limited to college campuses. Leaders are readers as well. Podcasts are what they listen to. Good leaders are forced to keep up with current events to remain relevant. I am here to tell you that I did not get credentialed until years after I had started my business and achieved the base level of success *(meaning I still had more work to do to reach my peak).*   But I didn't let that stop me from learning everything I could about my industry. Having those extra years of hands-on education provided me with the skills and knowledge I needed to make smarter decisions and become a more well-rounded person.

> **Decisiveness**

Making decisions will be one of your most important jobs as a leader. You won't always make the "correct" decisions, and there may be instances when there isn't one to make at all. However, when a decision must be made, you will be the one to make it, as well as the one who will feel the consequences and be held accountable for them. You won't do effectively when stressful situations demand immediate action if you procrastinate on making judgments or delegate complex decisions to others.

> **Passion**

Another important quality for a leader is passion. There's no denying that successful leaders and entrepreneurs are passionate about what they're doing. Your passion and enthusiasm will fuel your efforts as a leader, and your colleagues, partners, and customers will notice. Because enthusiasm is contagious, if you're genuinely enthusiastic about your business, the people around you will most likely be as well. For many leaders, passion also translates into charm, which helps them get greater media awareness. All of this is to say that starting a business based on your passion is far more enjoyable than starting a business based only on financial incentives.

FACTORS THAT CAN CHANGE

The qualities listed above do not guarantee that someone will be a good leader. Possessing those attributes displays potential, but every business is different, and effective leaders understand how to balance variable aspects to get the most out of their circumstances.

> ➢ **Styles of Leadership**

There are many various forms of leadership, and there is no one simple strategy. What your team expects, the culture you're attempting to create, and how you operate best all play a role in how one leads. Some businesses, for example, thrive under the leadership of a demanding boss who refuses to be told "no." Others thrive with a manager that is willing to compromise and allow staff to succeed on their own.

➢ **Oddities in the Industry**

Consider the industry you're seeking to break into and the size of your company as you improve your leadership talents. A law firm, for example, will need a severe and formal head, but a company that develops video games for children will need a more playful and laid-back boss. Small firms benefit from ground-level oversight and contact, but large organizations require executives that keep a distance from the bulk of employees and focus on the bottom line.

➢ **Changes in the Environment**

Changes in leadership trends and viewpoints should be considered by leaders. For example, a few decades ago, it was practically impossible for a CEO or boss to go into a conference wearing jeans and a sweatshirt. *No more stuffy suits and jackets!* Today, Mark Zuckerberg of Facebook and his Silicon Valley contemporaries have made it popular, allegedly to reduce decision fatigue. *And judging by his net worth, I think he's done something right here.*

➢ **There is no such thing as a "set in stone" situation.**

If you don't meet the above description of a leader, you may believe it's difficult to develop a successful company. However, the important takeaway here should not be determining whether you are now qualified for leadership or even which attributes you need to cultivate to become a leader. Instead, you should use this data to help you figure out your strengths and limitations. *There is no cookie-cutter method to it!* Leaders, just like everyone else, all have flaws, but the most effective ones try to improve those flaws while leveraging their strengths to overcome them. Any substantial flaws could be compensated for by a strong partner, employee, or mentor.

"

It's not the final destination that true radical leaders work towards; it's the opportunity to travel the path of continuous learning and growth that matters most.

DEVELOPING A SUCCESSFUL LEADER'S MINDSET

Sometimes we put too much focus on what the world has to say about value and execution, that we get attached to a game plan, without knowing that the only way to win is by setting your mind up to achieve what you want to achieve with that game plan. As a business leader, you are down in the trenches in the everyday details of your business's success. You get so caught up in worrying about your bottom line, your sales goals, or your next board meeting. Amid the chaos, it's easy to forget that intangibles -- like your beliefs and mindset -- play a significant role in your success.

When you change your mindset, achieving success and developing into a great leader is not something out of your league. You start to see new opportunities because your mind shifts to look at ways of how to increase your impact and grow your business and yourself.

The most successful entrepreneurs share a set of core beliefs that help them persevere as they grow their businesses. These four tips will promote a positive mindset and increase your chances of success as a leader:

1. Trust that you'll adapt to new challenges. Successful leaders approach uncertainty with confidence. When faced with an unfamiliar challenge, they think of similar situations they've handled before or skills sets that might apply. Focus on the abilities you do have and apply your general knowledge to whatever comes your way. If you focus on your current skills and your ability to learn new ones, you'll be less likely to feel overwhelmed.

2. Attribute your success to hard work, not luck. Successful leaders believe their achievements are due to hard work, not just lucky circumstances. That's the result of people who believe they've worked hard and trusted their ability to master new or unfamiliar skills. Leaders who are confident in their ability to learn are more likely to seek out and persevere through tough challenges, increasing their chances of success.

3. Believe that you are unique. Every great entrepreneur stands on the shoulders of giants, but successful leaders champion their individuality. In other words, they don't try to become the next Oprah Winfrey or Elon Musk. To be successful, learn from the people you admire but don't try to emulate them. If you foster the unique strengths that you bring to the table, then you will be far more likely to stand out in a crowded industry versus blending into it.

4. Challenge your negative beliefs. If you want to succeed, stomp out the invisible enemies that might be holding you back. Try not to self-handicap. For example, an executive who believes he won't meet his sales goals is more likely to prioritize other tasks, giving him a preemptive excuse for a mediocre performance. His belief becomes a self-fulfilling prophecy. Notice the goals or tasks that you shy away from and articulate your beliefs about them. Challenge any negative thoughts by reminding yourself that you will succeed if you apply yourself. When your beliefs are confident and positive, your actions will promote success.

Throughout your career, you can have dozens or even hundreds of these kinds of points where you can absorb insight. But you're not meant to sit down, put your feet up, and pacify your ego in any of them. Instead, you're simply meant to see how all those points interconnect and decide where you want to go next. And the more you travel the leadership path, the more comfortable you'll get with being malleable, both as a leader and in your general life. Uncertainty will lose its bite, you'll have more faith in your ability to adapt, and fearlessness will come more naturally.

"

With plenty of opportunities to learn, your confidence will certainly improve with time.

74

DEFINING AND DESIGNING YOUR LEADERSHIP STYLE

If success is truly what you are after, then being content to stay where you are is not even an option on the table. There must be a fearless desire for growth and progress to take on the forefront of your success journey as a leader. This is what we usually mean when we talk about becoming a leader or being on a leadership journey.

The big issue that I have with utilizing the word "journey" in the sense that we tend to use it for development, is that it implies that the journey – if you will – has some picture-perfect endpoint. So, when we slap this word onto leadership, it gives the impression that there's a final destination where you look a certain expected way, you're fully mature, and now you can go swim with the biggest fish. This is farthest from the true perspective when it comes to achieving success as a leader.

In the ever-evolving world of entrepreneurship, there's never a true endpoint to the leadership journey. There's never a final destination where you can nod your head and say you're done or that you're 100% sure you're prepared for everything. You don't know what you're going to end up doing or looking like. The transformation never stops.

DEFINING YOUR LEADERSHIP STYLE

There is no clear cut-and-dry definition for what being a great leader means. As with success, there is no one-size-fits-all methodology or leadership style that suits everyone the same. Leaders are like chameleons in that they can adapt to their surroundings and preferred environments. Therefore, determining what your signature leadership style is, is vital to the way you move forward on your success path.

Are you aware that there are six primary types of leaders? Read below and determine where you fit into the mold.

Coercive leaders *demand immediate compliance.* Also known as the Directive leadership style. The directive leadership style is where all the power is with the leader—it is highly centralized and undivided. Its adherents prefer giving commands and directives because they are unwilling to take any suggestions from those under them. While it is the most useful approach in a crisis situation or when managing a team that is not performing up to par, it is not a sustainable approach when it comes to managing people.

They are quick to assert authority and take charge of everything. Their sole objective is management, boundary setting, and task orientation rather than strictly relationship building. The pros to this style of leadership are that they are crystal clear in their communication and quick to make decisions as they are the sole decision-maker. The cons are that it can be tremendously counterproductive in settings that require team efforts because they come across as micromanagers and dictators.

Authoritative leaders *mobilize people toward a vision.* Also known as Visionary leadership. Authoritative leadership refers to a management style where the leader is in complete control. An authoritative leader is one who sets the goals, determines the processes, and oversees all steps it takes to reach those goals with little or no input from team members. Authoritative leadership drives organizations and their employees toward common goals. These types of leaders work with employees at every step of their processes, leading and coaching them to success.

This kind of leadership works well for meeting urgent needs quickly. It works best in emergencies that need a solution as soon as possible as it provides a much-needed productivity boost just before deadlines and improves decision-making during delays or similar situations. Authoritative leadership also works well in situations where there is little room for error. This type of leader may make fast decisions, but each one is highly effective.

On the flip side of the coin, for employees who are accustomed to having free reign over how they complete tasks, work toward company goals, and contribute to overhead, the prescriptive approach of the authoritative leadership style can appear somewhat overbearing.

Affiliative leaders *create emotional bonds and harmony.* An affiliative style of leadership puts people first, concentrating on creating a harmonious working environment and building emotional bonds. The affiliative leadership style requires lots of empathy and the ability to build relationships through a range of communication styles. This kind of leader is a caring nurturer who is tuned in closely to the emotions of the people around them. They care about performance and team members' abilities to achieve goals and objectives, but they are much more interested in how people are feeling in the workplace.

Affiliative leaders cultivate strong feelings of trust and togetherness, which can lead to improved innovation and creativity. Affiliative leaders also excel at improving flexibility in the working environment – they value freedom and trust that their people will employ methods that ensure success.

The downside to this leadership style is that affiliative leaders focus so much on the positive that they often overlook situations where below-average or mediocre performance needs to be addressed, yet because of their emotional attachment, they often struggle with delivering constructive feedback or addressing areas of concern. They also have a tendency to create environments in which there's a sense that mediocrity is tolerated or acceptable.

Democratic leaders *build consensus through participation.* Also known as participative leadership or shared leadership. Democratic leadership is when members of the group take a more participative role in the decision-making process. It can apply to any organization from private businesses to schools to the government. The key objective is to generate new ideas and solutions from a team using consensus and commitment.

While the democratic process tends to focus on group equality and the free flow of ideas, the leader of the group is still there to offer guidance and control. This leadership style is known to be one of the most effective types and leads to higher productivity, better contributions from group members, and increased group morale. However, it does have some potential downsides. In situations where roles are unclear or time is of the essence, democratic leadership can lead to communication failures and uncompleted projects. In some cases, group members may not have the necessary knowledge or expertise to make quality contributions to the decision-making process. Democratic leadership can also result in team members feeling like their opinions and ideas aren't considered, which may lower employee satisfaction and morale.

In order for this style to be effective, team members must be highly competent and understand the organizational vision very clearly.

Pacesetting leaders *expect excellence and self-direction.* Individuals who exhibit Pacesetting behaviors tend to have high-performance standards and work hard to ensure those standards are met. They are very results-driven and also tend to lead by example; however, the downfall is that they can be reluctant to delegate or collaborate because of concerns that others won't finish tasks to their satisfaction.

This leadership style can be effective in small group settings, research teams, or with a line-up of high-performance individuals who view the leader with respect---think professional athletics as an example. But it's important to note that this particular leadership gear can seize up quickly if the pacesetter steps in too frequently and tries to do it all, which can slow progress, creativity, and innovation.

Pacesetting leadership values results more than anything. This leadership style can be good to reach short-term results but can be detrimental to team engagement and motivation in the long run.

Coaching leaders *develop people for the future.* Coaching leadership is characterized by collaboration, support, and guidance. Coaching leaders strive to identify the unique strengths and weaknesses of their team and are focused on bringing out their best by guiding them through goals and obstacles that shape the skills to meet professional goals.

While the coaching leadership style is generally viewed as a positive and effective form of leadership, that doesn't necessarily mean it's the right fit for every leader or company. Coaching leaders don't tell people what to do. Instead, they seek to identify developmental gaps by guiding individuals to come to the right decisions or answers on their own using guided questions.

The cons of this leadership style is that it requires a great deal of time and energy due to its resource-intensive nature. Additionally, it may hinder the efficiency of getting results in a timely manner, which may not be the ideal choice for high-pressure or strictly results-driven companies and individuals.

Remember, you do not need to already be in a leadership role to begin developing a leadership style that is unique to who you are as an individual. After all, early preparation beats poor performance any day of the week!

DESIGNING YOUR LEADERSHIP PATH

The question now becomes "how do you find your unique leadership style?" I do not believe that there's no one shoebox that you should place yourself into. Contingent upon the level in which you're at on your success path can depict where you are and how you operate as a leader. Styles can evolve and anyone can grow to be an effective leader so long as they are able to adapt and adjust, as necessary.

A major component of the way many people approach leadership is that so much of business teaches you to focus so hard on managing risk. Is this a necessary part of the process? *Of course.* But somewhere along the way, we put our focus on the message that if we prepare just enough, we'll know how to resolve everything that comes our way. Thus, preparedness has become the focal point in how we handle the fear of loss, stress, adversity, and uncertainty that comes with entrepreneurship.

To step into the space of becoming a radical leader, you must accept that you won't always know how to solve or have the answer to everything. You must also admit that there are always going to be situations you didn't foresee or that you don't have the right information or resources to handle yet. *That's called humility.* But then you take that humility, commit to the shift, and allow others who are more seasoned to teach and support you along the way.

As an example, I recall the time when I first decided that I wanted to host my first big multi-day global empowerment conference. My goal was to provide a safe space for women to come together in sisterhood by uncovering the invisible enemies that prevented them from stepping into their light and jumpstart their healing journey from past trauma so that they can boldly become the successful leaders they deserved to be. *Sounds great, right?* I indeed had a great, well-thought-out plan for how to move things forward.

Because I thought I knew what to do, I dove right in. I hired an amazing keynote speaker, Lisa Nichols, and it was full speed ahead from there. Everything to facilitate an amazing conference was in place. But what I hadn't prepared for was how to handle the massive level of impact and transformation that was made in the room among the women. My well-thought-out plan of action turned into "wait, what the hell do I do now." I had accomplished the goal of getting them in the room and creating the transformation, but when the transformation happened, that became a whole new problem that I *wasn't* prepared for and *didn't* immediately know how to deal with.

In that situation, I suddenly doubted myself. I was afraid of failing. Fortunately, Lisa was there with me along for the ride. She had made her mark as a leader in the industry many years ago and traveled the transformation road a lot more than me. She helped me facilitate an amazing conference and execute my plan better. And by the end of the conference, I'd learned something critical that I knew would help me as I led in the future. If I had allowed ego to get in the way and not be receptive to learning from the greats, then I really would have failed at not only the conference but myself as a great leader in the making. I will never forget her words to me before she departed to return to California. She said, *"I admire your humility. You remind me of me when I first started in this space."* Can you imagine being told that by someone who *you* admire? I latched on to her teachings and used them to guide me into my greatness as a leader.

"

Preparedness doesn't make you fearless. Learning in humility does.

EVOLVING IN YOUR LEADERSHIP GREATNESS

In case you haven't figured it out by now, the best way to become a great leader is to get clear on who you are and what your core values are and start showing up in them daily. Chances are, as soon as you step into the role, you will be hit with hard choices and decisions that only you can resolve.

Becoming a leader is one thing; becoming a "great" leader, however, is a completely different ballgame. As an entrepreneur, at some point, your great idea and strategic vision will not be enough if your desired impact has not inspired people who are willing to follow you. This is a common "pitfall" over time, especially for those entrepreneurs who do not invest in developing their leadership skills or those who may take those skills for granted.

Great leadership is contingent upon one's ability to build a team of followers and apply their goals to turn them into leaders as well who understand your mission and business environmental module. And, of course, a great leader needs to always be ready for change coming from any direction without fear so that you can tackle it head-on.

More than likely, you will have to adjust your leadership methods based on your current situations and where you are at the moment. Here are five core tips to help you evolve as a great leader:

1. Know your value proposition

Be in tune with what your core strengths and weaknesses are from both your own and others' perspectives. Assessing yourself on your levels of compassion, integrity, and intuitiveness are very much key commonalities among great leaders. Then taking action to address any weaknesses is a key element of the leadership road ahead.

2. Assess your relationships

An outstanding leader ensures that each individual in their circle of influence can offer their best consistently. Know what matters to those on your team so that you can easily and properly engage them in helping you move things forward. A great leader will know who belongs and what they add to the table.

3. Maintain clear communication

Understanding and being clear about your core strengths and role, and consequently those of each of your team members, provide clarity in both who is doing what and how things should be done. This eliminates role confusion and overlapping, which in turn will increase productivity. This can be challenging for entrepreneurs who have to transition from being a solopreneur 'doing it all' to delegating to others.

4. Think strategically

Great leadership means being able to guide with an eye on the big goal. It also involves cultivating the ability to communicate a vision for balancing the urgency of the moment with future challenges and opportunities.

5. Be open and ready for change

Agility is a skill necessary at all levels of the organization. By default, entrepreneurs and great leaders alike are positioned to make decisions, implement, and test new practices, and adjust as results come in. Do not allow "perfect" to be the enemy of the great!

CLARIFYING YOUR CORE COMPETENCIES AS A LEADER

While there is no "one-size-fits-all" blueprint for becoming a great leader, in my experience, carving out a successful leadership plan of action would be critical and should include several elements such as assessing past performances and future responsibilities that are important growth and development areas. This should include both professional and personal objectives, goals, and aspirations for yourself, your business, and your circle of influence.

Now you can move forward in defining objectives and goals as they relate to you and your future leaders. Here are a few things to consider in this process:

- What are you trying to accomplish?
- How do you plan to accomplish each objective?
- Who and what involvement of others is needed to support the accomplishment of each objective? How can you best leverage your existing circle of influence? What changes do you need to make in terms of expanding the circle?
- Do you have quantitative evidence and detail of what is required to complete each objective? If not, what do you need to do to acquire it?
- What's the timeline for each objective to be accomplished? Are the milestones clearly defined and communicated to everyone with a role in the process?

Getting clarity on your leadership core competencies is an extremely important part of the process of becoming a great leader. Make sure that you include regular process reviews to get a clear understanding of how people perceive you as a leader – whether it's through your coaching sessions, peer-to-peer, or your circle. The goal is to clarify your areas of excellence and –most importantly– highlight opportunities for growth. Keep in mind that people follow inspiring leaders. Therefore, on a daily basis, be sure to inject something into your routine that ensures that you are pouring into your circle and giving them something to accomplish – and then hold them accountable to that task by following up and communicating.

A great way for leaders to gain perspective on who they are as a leader is to take a more objective look at what they believe defines their leadership style. This will not only assist you with the ability to adapt the way you lead to fit the environment you are in, but also lend more perspective to how you build your legacy of leaders going forward.

The most important part of your entrepreneurial venture is you. And if you've ever tried to write your own biography, you know that it's one of the more difficult things to do when it comes to identifying your characteristics in an objective manner. This is where the SWOT analysis comes into play. SWOT is used to help individuals take a more objective approach to evaluate themselves or a new venture by analyzing **strengths, weaknesses, opportunities**, and **threats**. Using this method as a way to see yourself through your own lens will only better position you to become the best possible leader you can be.

Strengths

Strengths in the SWOT analysis are the attributes that are considered to be necessary for the ultimate success of a business or individual. This segment is used to define our future paths and allow us to see where we add the most value. Knowing where our positive attributes lie highlights the areas where we can be poised for success.

Look at Steve Jobs. He was a design genius and made visually stunning products the hallmark of his leadership at Apple and Pixar. His attention to detail and persistent iteration helped form his legacy, and in turn, has improved standards for the broader tech industry.

Or take me for example. I've always been extremely persistent and goal-oriented. Growing up, I loved to read – primarily teen fiction and love stories. I would visit the library or the bookmobile (which was a library on wheels that would ride through the neighborhoods for people to check out and purchase books), but I would check out books, take them home and edit them to change the narrative of the story to make it more appealing. As a result, I ended up writing and publishing six books of my own that would grant me the honor of becoming a 3x International Bestselling Author. This experience as a young adult revealed to me early on that my creativity and persistence could lead to great achievements. Identifying my personal strengths defined my career and helped me discover that my greatest potential to excel would be in founding my own publishing company.

While your strength might not be a fastidious eye for design or dogged determination, it's likely something equally as important to your success as a leader. Take time to think back on moments of success in your life, put on your ego-centric hat, and figure out exactly how you got there. Those traits are likely what will also drive your success as an entrepreneurial leader.

Weaknesses

The factors within the SWOT analysis formula that could prevent successful results within a project are *Weaknesses*. Weaknesses can derail the process before it even begins. It's equally important to take an honest and objective look at your shortcomings. This isn't about putting yourself down, but more so to identify areas for improvement where you can either focus on growth.

Mark Zuckerberg, for example, is an incredible visionary thinker when it comes to the future of human connection and communication, but he relies on someone else to manage the operational future of Facebook. This doesn't make Zuckerberg any less of a leader -- it makes him an even better one.

Ironically, my greatest weakness lies within this very notion of relying on my peers. As a perfectionist, I often struggle with trusting others to complete tasks at my high standards. Identifying this has allowed me not only to surround myself with a talented team of people I trust, but to give them space to operate fully in their assigned roles.

Identifying weaknesses requires complete honesty, transparency, and some tough self-love. Think of moments you've experienced challenges or moments of great stress and identify what you could have done better or differently in the process. While there may have been external issues out of your direct control, it's possible that you lacked a particular skill to succeed in the situation. By identifying those weaknesses early on, you can proactively address them or seek support from others, ultimately making you a better leader.

Opportunities

Opportunities are often classified as external elements that might be helpful in achieving forecasted goals. These factors could involve individuals who wish to collaborate with you to help achieve success or the positive perception of you by the general public. Whereas the S and W of the matrix require internal reflection, opportunities don't always come from within. Oftentimes it takes an outside injection of innovation to mix up your perspective and have the greatest impact.

As the founder and CEO of multiple businesses, mountains of everyday stress make it difficult to get out of my head and focus on anything unrelated to my business. Meditation and some form of physical activity have become an important catalyst to clearing my mind, get a refresh, and invest my energy in something other than my day-to-day.

Opportunity is the external influence that can come from almost anywhere -- your family, a book that you're reading, or your hobbies. Inspiration is more likely to strike when you take a step back, so it's important to get outside of the office and discover what the world around you has to offer.

Threats

Threats can come from external elements beyond our control, like starting a company only to have a recession hit or having a personal tragedy dry up your resources. While these external factors can gravely affect your success and threaten your progress, they may actually be your best resources for inspiration and can encourage you to push the limits of success.

The most important lesson I've gained from times of stress is the value of mindfulness and calmness. This is where my meditation really comes in handy in helping me relax my mind and get clear on what I need to do next. You will undoubtedly face countless setbacks as an entrepreneur and leader, but by leaning into your vision with a clear head and direction, those setbacks will be possible to overcome. Trusting in this process allows for something that all entrepreneurs are looking for – a structured way to creatively think about improvement.

My good friend, Elon Musk, for example, started out in fintech with PayPal and is now revolutionizing travel with Tesla and SpaceX. The role of tech founder/CEO is increasingly greater than just leading one successful company. It's about being a visionary that extends past immediate projects to look for future innovations. Companies can come and go, but great leadership is everlasting. Leveraging a SWOT analysis of your own management style could be the key to make that move from good to great.

By the way, I do not *really* know Elon personally, but it did make the read a little more exciting!

"

Leadership and learning are indispensable to each other.

EXCLUSIVE INTERVIEW WITH LIFE STRATEGIST, TAWAWN LOWE

WOW! I still can't believe it's been over 15 years since we first made our acquaintance. You were just getting into the coaching space and figuring out your brand. And fast forward to now – you've grown tremendously into a staple figure in the empowerment space. Thank you for taking a moment to shine a light on entrepreneurship and share your personal experiences and wisdom with new and aspiring leaders reading this book.

Please give us an overview of your success journey and how you managed both a full-time job and running a successful business(es).

In 2007, I started Tawawn Lowe Coaching which has evolved over the years, and now is Tawawn Lowe Enterprises which serves as the umbrella for the TLConsultancy, Tea Lover's Café, TLC-Publishing Company, and the Women Walking in Their Own Shoes Movement. In 2015, I started the Women Walking in Their Own Shoes Foundation and being the owner of multiple businesses and a full-time worker has been challenging. Learning how to manage multiple businesses, and time management was the biggest problems. There were many sleepless nights, missed deadlines, missed opportunities, money lost, loss of clients, disappointments, and failures. But there also were great victories, shifts that lead to new business opportunities, new clients, and wins with my individual and corporate clients. For the first year, I did not make a consistent $5,000 in all my businesses combined, and I had no clue of how to shift the trajectory.

In 2012, I broke down, and I decided to dissolve Tawawn Lowe Coaching. I went into prayer and sought God for the answer to my next. The answer was not what I expected. Not only did God say not to dissolve, but to start a movement – Women Walking in Their Own Shoes, and to kick the movement off with a Conference. In my praying and fighting God, he dropped the answer in my spirit why my businesses were not yielding a greater harvest. The shift to elevate my business was right in front of my face. The revelation was simple. The shift in my business took place in October 2012, when I had my first conference, published my first book, and changed the focus of my service and business model. My first client was myself, and I took 2-months to construct a goal position system (GPS) that outlined each one of my businesses, outlining how much I wanted to make in each business, the services to be offered, how many events, clients were required to generate the desired income. I started my new year with my GPS that provide me clarity and direction. There still were some bumps in the road but the outsourcing and delegation with the system put in place allowed for a less bumpy ride.

Balancing a full-time job and running my business is still challenging, but I am well worth the award. When I think of quitting, I remember my why. I would never lie and say it easy, but I would say that learning what motives you, being self-aware, developing effective success habits and principles, you too can make them both work.

What motivates you?

Motivation is a tricky multifaceted thing because what motivates you today, can be different a year from now. I can truly say there is a multitude of things that motivates me. However, when I think about what consistently brings me personal and professional satisfaction, and truly makes my baby jump is helping other, visible results, and being a champion for the underdog. These three elements are my motivation and play a significant part in how I lead.

God gives us many gifts, one of my mines is the gift of services, and this particular gift is directly aligned to my purpose. Helping others has always been important to me, and as I have evolved personally and professionally, it has become not only my purpose but one of my biggest motivations. The ability to aid in the service of others, and minimize their pain brings me great satisfaction. It motivates me to look for different approaches in which I can influence, undertake, make an impact, and give back.

My gift of service – giving back has shaped and motivated who I'm still becoming, how I show up in the world and created my legacy. My motivation to help others has manifested itself in my various roles, and my works. As an Evangelist giving back has motivated my role as a missionary, my mission work, and the ministries in which I lend my gifts and talents. My giving back has influenced my community services efforts, the charities I work with, my philanthropy endeavors through my former and current non-profit organization, and my becoming a certified life coach. Each one of my roles and endeavors motivates me to embrace my gift of service, and to continue to think of diverse ways to give back to others. Know that I have the power to make a difference is my motivation.

They say seeing is believing is true. I don't know about you, but when I can see the things, I have achieved, the influence I made, and changes that come from my contributions, that shit turns me on. This is why visible results are one of my biggest motivations. There is nothing greater for me than seeing my latest book pop-up in a Google search for major outlets such as Barnes and Nobles, seeing somebody read the book, seeing an organization submit and pay an invoice for my service, holding awards in my hand for my efforts, reading testimonies from a client, or seeing my clients win and manifest their goals or any results from my work. I have learned and teach my clients and mentees how to use visible results as tangible evidence of their achievements. Tangible evidence is important because it boosts self-esteem and confidence, proves you can do it, measures how far you have come, and serve as a great reminder when you need that extra motivation. Visible results are the gift that keeps on giving when you learn how to see beyond results and see all the benefits.

Nothing puts a fire in spirit more than the desire to prove naysayers wrong. Because of this, self-identifying as an underdog has become my secret weapon. Instead of seeing the underdog (myself) as a negative, I transformed that mindset into a positive. The secret weapon is turning others' doubt, including my own into your motivation. Seeing myself as the underdog now works like motivational rocket fuel for me. Regardless of how much success I achieve, my self-determination and mental toughness are fortified by viewing myself as never being more than the cafeteria worker, the "comeback queen." My inspiration for championing the underdogs is directly connected to my backstory. One of my biggest success lessons has been proving others' self-limited beliefs about me wrong. Now, I understand the only person you need to prove yourself to is yourself. However, I have found great inspiration in showing people better than I can tell them. As a coach and mentor, I show my clients and mentees how to adopt a mindset growth that can increase their self-motivation, effectiveness, and success. This includes offering them the perspective of turning others' doubt into their motivation. And how they can thrive by proving their naysayers (which include themselves) wrong can be fuel to drive success.

What do you believe are the core qualities of a leader and why?

Self-awareness, self-esteem, self-confidence, and self-worth are intertwined and have a significant impact on one's outlook and belief about themselves. I believe every leader should have a good conscious awareness of their thoughts, feeling, and attitudes about themselves and their abilities. In leading people, the leader needs to possess a healthy level of self-assurance that is cultivated from self-understanding, a high belief in themselves, their ability, and skills, and understanding their worth. It is hard to be in authority when you don't believe in yourself. People can see and smell when you are not confident.

All good leaders understand the importance of transparency and that it is a key attribute in their communication. Understanding how to honestly and effectively communicate changes, key information, and intentions allows individuals to trust their leadership. Leadership who exercises transparency understands there is a time and a way to convey information. They are aware of how new information may impact people, so they impart it with care, understanding the time of delivering critical information, and demonstrate empathy and respect in their communication.

Leaders have a great responsibility to communicate, creating, maintaining, and keeping their eye on the prize (vision of their company or organization). The vision is at the forefront of their decision-making, employing foresight to plan for obstacles and driving changes. Moving the company or organization towards the vision is vital, but being a visionary is also a core quality of a leader. Great leadership qualities also included being a visionary, be able to see beyond the present looking into how they can take the company or organization into the next decade.

Valuing people is important. Some of the best things a leader can do is show respect, bolster confidence, empower to succeed, and understand the importance of recognition of the people they lead. Great leader invests in other serving as a mentor and coach to assist other with achieving their next level of success.

What – in your opinion – is the difference between passion and purpose and how does it correlate to achieving success?

Yes, I truly believe there is a difference between passion and purpose. I define passion as being those things that I like, and sometimes love to do, that bring joy and excitement to my life. I believe we all have a multitude of passions, and that our passions are fleeting, and evolve as we do. Passion and purpose have some interconnection, but everything we are passionate about is not a part of our purpose. I know for me, some of my passions are where I find peace and solace, help me to relax, and serve a great purpose towards my self-love and self-care. We all heard the saying, "do what you love, and you'll never work a day in your life." That is a lie straight from the pit of hell. Everything you are passionate about is not always connected to your calling or purpose. One of my greatest passions is cooking. In the past, I have used this passion to create another source of income. I figure because I love doing, I should make money doing it. My business as a caterer only lasted two years. The joy of cooking was lost in the demands of meeting other people's needs. It no longer felt like a choice, but more of a burden.

Purpose for me is your why – why you were created. I truly believe we all were created on purpose with a purpose, and part of our assignment is to identify that purpose. I see purpose as the way we use our God-given gifts, talents, and strengths to bring forth change, make a difference in this world, earn income, create a legacy, and edify the kingdom. For me, purpose is composed of many factors with passion being a part of the factors.

What are your core success habits and principles?

My core success habits and principles for success are the power of visualization, goal setting, embracing failure, asking for help, and me time that consists of prayer/mediation/affirmation, and not in that order. I truly believe how you start your day sets the tone for how you navigate your day. Your attitude and expectations are important and the atmosphere for positivity and success needs to be established. I start each day with a 30-minute routine that includes tea, scripture, prayer, affirmation, and/or mediation. This allows me to be centered on what I want to focus on for the day, give thanks to my creator, share my desires and fears, ask for wisdom and guidance, and to meditate on words and affirmations to bring forth mindfulness for my day. I also use this same principle/habit before going to bed. It allows me to release worry, give my doubts and fears to God, journal my day, and practice gratitude for what the day brought. Even if the day was not the best, I find gratitude in making it through the day.

One of my biggest core success principles is the power of visualization – using the power of visualization to create your life and business vision, facilitate change, be creative. I believe we all should have a big picture (vision) for our lives to give us clarity and direction in all areas of life. Having a vision for my life also provides a framework for the goals needed to manifest my vision. I also use the power of visualization to create and identify new ways of doing business and to problem-solve. To support this principle, 10-years ago I started creating vision boards. I use the vision boards to keep my eyes on my dreams, to serve as motivation, and a reminder of my why.

All goals must be written say the experts, and they are right. I believe fully in writing the vision and making it clear. Therefore, goal setting is a big part of my success habits and principles. My goals are the playbook that supports my life and business vision outlines what is necessary to manifest the dream and keeps track of my small and big achievements. To support this principle, I set my goals in 90-day increments. This allows me to eat the elephant in small chunks, consistently reviewing the progression of my efforts, make changes as necessary, and keep my next steps in front of me.

This probably sounds crazy to some, but those who understand success will get it. Embracing failure is one of my top three success principles. Failure is a good teacher that provides constructive feedback. Failure is that part of success most people don't talk about. Failure has been a very good teacher over the years, and as I do self-assessments, one of the things I look at is my failures. I allow failure to be part of my motivation to keep trying. See you can't fail if you never try. Most importantly, I use failure to identify my weakness and what went wrong. Identifying my weakness teaches me what needs strengthening, and what went wrong allows me to visualize and explore what to do differently. Failure is a good teacher if you are willing to find the positive in the process.

Asking for help is hard, especially for women. Being a full-time worker and entrepreneur has taught me that I cannot do this alone, I need help. I will confess that some of my failures have resulted from me not having the resources needed to accomplish the task. In addition, to the crazy mindset that I can do this alone, or that can't anybody do it the way I do. This type of mindset and lack of resources is a recipe for failure. It took me almost three years in business to outsource for help and to ask those who could help. This was a big struggle in my personal, professional, and business life. Learning to ask for help required a mind shift, letting go of control, and trusting others to support my vision.

What is the best advice that you could lend to a new/aspiring entrepreneur? And how does it resonate with you personally?

The best advice I could lend to any new or aspiring entrepreneur is to *define who you want to become, how you want to show up in the world,* and *identify what you want for your life.* These factors are the key to your happiness, peace, and success. Let personal development be a lifetime journey, don't stop learning about yourself because self-awareness will be key at any level of success. Define success on your own terms, self-invest, don't allow other people's limiting beliefs to define you and what you can achieve. Trust that feeling in your gut, listen to those small whispers that speak to you, learn to be still, believe in something bigger than yourself, don't look for people to do or give what you won't do for yourself. Fall in love with you and love yourself unconditionally and let your love for yourself be honored in how you take care of yourself. Don't be scared to dream big, don't chase your dreams and aspiration, but catch them and do the work to manifest them. Never stop believing in yourself, even when the world seems like it's giving up on you. When you fall, get back up, and try again, and again. Remember that this is your life to create, and the sum of who you become is based on what you believe about yourself and your abilities. You are 100% percent responsible for your life.

The above resonates with me because I spent half of my life making someone else's limited belief about me, a self-fulfilling prophecy. I allowed that self-fulfilling prophecy to rob me of my power, diminish my self-confidence, and lead me to wander through my life with no vision or direction. It wasn't until I answered the three questions above, that I was able to accept responsibility for my life and stop blaming others.

Tawawn Lowe is the CEO of TLConsultancy, LLC, the Founder of the Women Walking in Their Own Shoes Movement and Foundation, the sole proprietor of Tea Lovers Cafe and TLC Publishing Company.

She serves as a bestselling author, philanthropist, transformational life strategist, and mentor.

Tawawn uses her multidimensional consulting and coaching practice to help her clients be intentional about their being and connect their life or business visions with goals to achieve success by way of accountability, facilitation, inspiration, coaching, and other dynamic mechanisms. She has combined her life experiences of navigating limited self-belief and fear of success, 25+ years of professional experience, and multiple certifications consisting of Life Coach certification, MBTI Certified Practitioner, Prosci ADKAR Change Management, and Facilitation Specialist to bring forth change, transformation to individuals, and organizations. Tawawn is inherently committed to the emboldening of women, specifically women 40+ desperately seeking greater fulfillment and purpose for the next chapter of their life.

To connect with Tawawn, visit www.tawawnlowe.com

"

Don't allow other people's limiting beliefs to define you and what you can achieve.

~ Tawawn Lowe

THE PILLARS OF GREAT LEADERSHIP

Many people think that leadership – in its simplest form, is but a title. Contrary to widely held belief, not everyone is cut out to lead no more than they can be deemed a leader. Leadership is earned and based on certain demonstrated criteria and abilities that make up this determinability. Certain individuals can impact the lives of others with their *actions*, like that of Dr. Martin Luther King, who inspired an entire generation of African Americans to march for their civil rights; *knowledge*, like Steve Jobs, whose innovations gave Apple the foundation it needed to dominate the smartphone market; and *words,* like the late great Nelson Mandela, who led a movement against the apartheid government in South Africa to achieve greater peace and fight for the removal of the racial injustices in the country. Their drive and passion for a cause greater than themselves inspired others to follow them.

Aside from leading through the aforementioned ways, great leadership is an essential catalyst for growing and guiding a company to the next level using unique expertise, insight, and innate abilities. I believe, based on personal knowledge and experience, that a great entrepreneurial leader possesses very distinct characteristics that set them apart and make them stand out from everyone else. *Does this imply that people are born leaders?* While it is very true that some people are born with the traits of a leader, others develop the traits from learned behavior and application. Let's delve into some of these leadership traits.

One thing that I know for sure is that leaders become successful because they hold themselves accountable. *Leaders take accountability.* What sets them apart is that they are known for challenging the status quo by refusing to surrender to the cards they are dealt. They are constantly striving to improve themselves and become true game-changers. Known for walking to the beat of their own drum and taking matters into their own hands, they do not allow others to dictate their paths or allow negative thoughts and circumstances to prevent them from taking the next steps in their lives; unlike many others who opt for comfortability and dormancy – existing in a life where they never realize their true potential. Leaders also take ownership of the people and environment in which they intervene. But this does not mean that leaders do everything themselves. Good leaders have mastered the art of delegation. A common mistake many leaders make is relegating rather than delegating. *Let me break that down.* When you relegate, you abandon your responsibility, which in turn diminishes your stance as a leader. When you delegate, you shape the outcome by allowing someone else to implement the actual task, while you are still taking responsibility for the outcome of it.

Another trait of a great leader is the *ability to empower others.* It is no secret that we as a people have the innate desire to belong – whether it's in a specific culture, class of people, tribe, or community. There is a longing deep within us to be a part of something bigger and greater than ourselves. Therefore, when a leader appears who shows us a way to be better not only as individuals but also as part of something larger collectively, it generates in us a sense of self-confidence. This self-confidence is, at its core, truly empowering and helps to mend a bridge from where we are to where we desire to be and believe we should be. A great leader knows how to empower others to see themselves in a bigger light that pushes them outside of their comfort zone and into their greatness. *"A leader is not measured by how far they have advanced themselves, but rather by how well they have advanced in the lives of others."*

Moreover, not only does a great leader empowers others as mentioned above, but they are also clearly *defined by a purpose* that is much bigger than themselves. When that purpose serves the greater good, it becomes the platform for great leadership. I am drawn to the quote by the great William Shakespeare, *"The meaning of life is to find your gift. The purpose of life is to give it away."* That one statement speaks volumes about how he chose to share his message to change the world by writing poetry that covered all human emotions and inspire works of other authors globally. That was his purpose and how he reached the masses. When you have a purpose that goes beyond yourself, people will see it and identify with it. Being driven by purpose defines the nobility of one's character. Simply put, purpose is the difference between a used car salesperson and a leader, and in the end, the leader is the one who makes the biggest impact on the world.

Finally, great leaders *have compassion and care for others*. To me, this is by far the hallmark of a great leader. Showing compassion towards others is not about a photo op, words on paper, or face you make; but an inherent characteristic that others can feel and hear when they are in your presence. Compassion comes alive through the warmth and timbre of your voice and the level of action one performs for the benefit of others. Compassion is selfless and a pure genuine concern for others. Great leaders have the fervent desire to connect with others on a deeper level and really get to know who they are at their core. This is the best way for them to encourage others to be the best that they can be. In its most genuine form, compassion is woven into everything you do.

"

Leaders become great not because of their power, but because of their ability to empower others.

~John C. Maxwell

THINGS SUCCESSFUL ENTREPRENEURS AVOID THAT YOU NEED TO EMULATE

What we don't do is frequently more important than what we do. It is unquestionably true for those who achieve the pinnacle. Success does not happen by chance, and those who want to achieve it are certain about the habits, activities, and processes they avoid.

While the courage to keep going is something that many of us lack at times, any successful entrepreneur's journey demonstrates that they have tremendous guts, strong will, and grits *(not the kind you eat)*.

A crucial trait of a successful entrepreneur is a "never give up" mindset. Regardless of the circumstances, their zeal is unquenchable. They never give up, even in the face of adversity or defeat. I used to get asked quite frequently during my battle with cancer, "how do you do it? How do you keep going and still put the needs of others ahead of your own while you are fighting for your life? And honestly, it was such an easy thing for me to do as a leader and successful business owner. I had people who depended on my expertise and my encouragement and motivation – it was their anchor. And that's what great leaders do. Even amid adversity, we do not give up on ourselves or others.

Let's look at several things that every great entrepreneurial leader refuses to do in this chapter. I hope these tips will help you stay motivated as you embark on your entrepreneurial adventure.

1. Responding to emails as soon as possible

Successful entrepreneurs aren't passively waiting for distractions in front of their laptops. Because their mind is elsewhere, they aren't checking their emails every ten minutes. Rather than being tugged in different directions by pings and requests daily, they are batching their responses to free up time for genuine work.

It's partially because they have other things to do and partly because they don't want to train those around them to expect rapid responses. Maybe they'll respond in a day or two; maybe they won't respond at all. So, it puts the responsibility on the sender to craft an email that is worth responding to.

To remain on task, I include the task of checking and responding to emails on my daily calendar and task list three times daily – morning (at the start of my work hour), afternoon (either right before or right after lunch), and of course, evening (at the end of my workday). This helps me to not only regulate my productivity time but also sets the tone for how I do business and communicate with others.

2. Allowing anyone to make a reservation on their calendar

Have you ever tried to schedule a meeting with Jeff Bezos directly on his calendar? Have you ever sent Oprah a calendar invitation?

They have gatekeepers after gatekeepers work to clear and secure their time to concentrate on their duties. An open diary with free slots every day indicates that your time can be snatched away from you in a moment, and your week can be thrown aside. What is the goal?

Only the best, most obvious "hell yeah" possibilities will be blocked out by successful entrepreneurs. It's on their terms, not the terms of others. You can't just "jump on a call" without a plan or a cause, or until they've requested it, not the other way around. The exclusivity serves to reinforce the fact that they are not wasting their time.

One of my core success habits in this regard is regulating my calendar. I set aside specific amounts of time for very specific types of meetings. For example, if you have another entrepreneur who wants to speak with you regarding a collaborative opportunity, open an appointment type called Business Development (or whatever you identify with) and set 1 to 2 hours of availability maybe 2 or 3 days per week for people to book on your appointment calendar. Most apps like Acuity Scheduling will allow you to attach a pre-booking questionnaire to the appointment that they must complete before selecting a date on your calendar. This way, you will know the basics of the appointment before getting on the call and saving yourself some time in determining whether it is worth the 20 minutes or not. I use this method for new client

Discovery Sessions so that I am not inundated with a bunch of people wasting my time.

3. Taking the phone call

Successful entrepreneurs are planners who have a clear idea of what they want to accomplish each day. That is the default setting. Calls for "just two minutes" or "to pick your brain" are unlikely to be returned. They aren't disrespectful; they don't want to be caught off guard, and a phone call would require a direct answer, which they don't want to offer. *Truth be told, no one gets to "pick my brain" for free. But I'll reserve this portion for another chapter.*

There aren't many true crises. Someone else's emergency isn't always the same as yours. Because successful people don't confuse urgent with important, it's easier for them to dismiss urgent requests in favor of going on with their plans. This does not give off the impression that you are being rude or ignoring them, however, look at it as a way of reclaiming your time and teaching people how to do business with you.

An effective way to protect your phone time is to eliminate making your personal or business cell readily accessible by perhaps using a Google number – which is free. This number can be connected to your personal cell phone but offers its own voicemail and text messaging system. This way you can state your business hours and offer contact instructions for pressing matters.

4. Taking advantage of social media

When successful entrepreneurs use social media, they do it to create rather than consume. They aren't scrolling through their home feed or clicking on the Explore option. They are unlikely to see your Instagram story. Consumption of social media is neither work nor play; it falls somewhere in the center.

Successful entrepreneurs understand that you can take the finest parts of everything, including social media, and leave out the bad. They treat it as if it were a tool. You can keep your audience up to date on your work, life, and thoughts without becoming distracted.

Now I know this is hard for a lot of people. They feel like social media keeps them knowledgeable of the latest goings-on. However, it has been known to be one of an entrepreneur's biggest hindrances. So how do we combat this while still ensuring that we get that daily post and scroll in? I limit my time on social media to 1 hour per day. *How in the hell do you do this?* I can hear you asking me that question. So here goes. I schedule time on my calendar for social media. Twenty minutes – three times per day. In the morning, I will post on all platforms and then review/respond to comments from the day before. In the afternoon, I will review/respond to comments from the morning posts. And my final twenty minutes of posting and commenting is done in the evening after work. Of course, you can hire a social media manager to do this for you if you want to pay hundreds of dollars per month.

Another very effective way to manage this is to use a social media scheduling app like Hootsuite or Social Bee. You can load up and schedule your content to post on specific days and times. Then all you would need to do is go online to engage your audience. *Surely all you would need is 15-20 minutes to do this throughout the day ...* you can do it!

5. Wasting Time

Successful entrepreneurs understand and respect the value of time and refuse to waste it. They will also not squander your time. They won't bother you with frivolous requests, nor do we jump at every opportunity that comes our way.

While it's great to be in demand and a go-to in your industry, understanding that not every opportunity is the right fit for your purpose, business, or path is key when factoring in time and boundaries of your time. The last thing you want is to have your success journey filled with things that do not aid in or contribute to its actual success.

It's okay to screen your potential partnerships and even more okay saying "no" to things that are of no benefit to you.

6. Giving Up

Most of us find it difficult to recover from a failure or setback. Repeated setbacks can make us completely despondent about continuing down a specific path as many will react pessimistically instead of optimistically. However, as an entrepreneur, you cannot adopt this attitude as it will only hinder your progress.

Successful entrepreneurs, on the other hand, are not afraid of failure as they understand that behind each obstacle or setback is an opportunity to gain experience, improve, or learn a valuable, much-needed lesson. Rather, they accept it as merely a part of what comes with the entrepreneur territory.

7. Being conceited

True entrepreneurs don't get carried away with their success. In fact, they are extremely humble. They refuse to be arrogant, even when they are extremely successful and wealthy. Arrogance will not help you acquire people's love and respect. Humility, on the other hand, is highly valued and admired.

8. Making a lot of excuses

Entrepreneurs that succeed are self-aware. They've done a comprehensive assessment of themselves and are fully aware of their strengths and weaknesses.

They stay faithful to themselves and their surroundings. If they make a mistake, they accept full responsibility and seek to correct it as soon as possible. They don't blame others or make excuses for themselves.

9. Investing in Perfection.

There is no such thing in business – or life for that matter, as perfection and nobody understands this better than entrepreneurs. The reality usually always turns out to be a little different than expected and you would be doing a huge disservice to yourself if you think otherwise. Successful entrepreneurs aren't obsessed with doing things exactly as planned because unbelievably, perfection is a silent killer of success as it hinders forward progression.

Instead, they understand that imperfection and making mistakes is normal and a healthy part of the process. If you wait until your product is in that "ideal" state before launching it, it may never happen. Entrepreneurs who succeed refuse to wait for things to be perfect. Imagine the stress-free life you'd have if you launched and did not beat yourself up because a mishap occurred, or if you did it "imperfectly" and realized that it worked out perfectly in the end. *Hmmm ...*

10. Trying to please Everyone

Successful entrepreneurs understand that they will never be able to please everyone. People will always be skeptical, critical, or distrustful of your conduct. There will, however, be those who believe in you as well.

Successful businesspeople are unconcerned about satisfying everyone. They aren't afraid to make a potentially controversial decision if they believe it is the right one.

11. Paying Attention to What Others Are Saying

Entrepreneurs who succeed are initiative-taking and driven. They don't seek out others' approval or permission. However, it's also important to not get engulfed in one way of thinking as it relates to communicating and getting constructive feedback from others.

It is important not to be so stuck in your ways of how you do business that your model is too rigid for growth and expansion. Successful entrepreneurs are constantly and consistently in student mode so that they can hear and learn from the valuable feedback and perspectives they receive.

12. Keeping a grudge

Holding a grudge against someone is believed to allow them to dwell rent-free in your thoughts. Holding grudges wastes valuable energy that may otherwise be put to better use.

Successful entrepreneurs understand that they have a finite amount of mental space. As a result, they only put what is important in it and refuse to allow others to take up mental space.

13. Making Value Compromises

For the sake of a quick win, successful entrepreneurs never compromise their ideals. However, they don't believe in breaking the rules when it comes to ethics and moral standards. They believe in conducting business ethically. Even if it takes them longer to succeed, they never compromise their moral compass or engage in unethical behavior. Remember, your reputation is all you have in business and a good one will take you very far.

14. Always maintaining a serious demeanor.

Successful business people don't believe in being solemn all the time. However, a little lighthearted joking can make everyone's work atmosphere less stressful and more pleasurable.

Unwinding is essential for successful entrepreneurs. They understand how it can energize and motivate individuals. As a result, they refuse to be always solemn.

15. Evaluating Their Success

Constantly evaluating or benchmarking your efforts and success can be detrimental rather than beneficial. Everyone develops at his or her rate.

Of course, you must be aware of your competitors and understand what needs to be done to expand. However, continuously comparing yourself to your colleagues or competitors and their growth rates is pointless.

As a result, successful entrepreneurs refuse to compare themselves to others. Instead, they focus on the big picture and their objectives.

16. Lighting Both Ends of the Candle

Successful entrepreneurs understand the importance of maintaining their health. As a result, they avoid working so hard that they get physically and psychologically exhausted.

They assume that investing time in something soothing at the end of the day will recharge their batteries. They also get enough sleep to wake up rejuvenated and ready to face the new day.

These practices may not come naturally to some of us. However, if you want to be a successful entrepreneur, you must learn these skills as soon as possible. They will not only enable you to overcome any negative ideas or sentiments, but they will also improve your attitude, ensuring that you are fully motivated.

Are you going about your day and business as if you want to be the person you want to be? Protect your personal space, concentrate on the needle-moving task you were sent here to do, avoid being on call, and regard time as the valuable and irreplaceable resource that it is.

ENTREPRENEURSHIP STRATEGIES THAT WORK

An entrepreneur might easily feel overwhelmed in today's ever-changing business atmosphere. It's critical, however, to stay focused on the company's objectives.

Even if they have a solid strategy in place, every entrepreneur should follow these six steps to ensure their success:

1. Research your competitors.

As a business owner, you must be aware of your competitors. You should also be aware of the competing product or services on the market.

2. No matter how successful your company is, save money.

To put it another way, live as cheaply as possible.

To deal with any tough patches that may come, entrepreneurs should be as conservative with their money as possible. Having several months' worth of operating expenditures in the bank will help you weather the most unexpected events.

3. Conduct market research on new products and services.

Learn about new products or services on the horizon that could help your organization run more smoothly.

Make sure you finish your homework. Are you utilizing all that technology has to offer? Is there an app that can help you better manage your time or service that allows you to delegate routine activities to free up time for more important projects?

4. Don't go after big markets right away.

During the early phases of your business, avoid growing into enormous marketplaces. It's possible that thinking "if we can merely grab 1% of China" is a mistake. However, if you keep three things in mind, niche marketing can be incredibly cost-effective:

- By providing something new and compelling, you can meet the market's specific needs.
- Know how to communicate with the market and what its triggers are.

Even minor components of a marketing strategy, such as the company's motto, should be in tune with that niche.

5. Pay attention to customer input and make changes as needed.

The proverb "always be closing," abbreviated ABC, is well-known among salespeople. Always Be Adapting, or ABA is an abbreviation used by entrepreneurs.

Entrepreneurs, on the other hand, can only evolve their businesses by listening to client input. It may not matter if one consumer dislikes your product, but if this is the case for a large number of customers and they're asking for a different feature, pay attention and be willing to adapt.

Pay attention to customer input while making changes to your marketing strategy, streamlining a product, or responding to the latest trends. Be ready to listen. This knowledge will enable you to promote your product or service better to stand out, perhaps even by exploiting your competitors' flaws.

6. Be adaptable to change.

Change is unavoidable in business, and those who can adapt are adaptable and versatile.

An entrepreneur must be willing to accept change and adjust his or her business operations, as necessary. Be adaptable. Don't be left behind if your product or service requires a change. Recognize that where you are now is unlikely to be where you will end up. Customers, profitability, and even business failure can all be affected by a lack of adaptation.

Recognize that the world is changing at a quick pace as an entrepreneur. Even a company that was created a year ago has the potential to affect the world today.

Yes, world leaders such as Bill Gates and Oprah Winfrey are frequently praised. Nonetheless, there is enough room in the game for everyone. Emerging market entrepreneurship could very well be a major element in the revival of a robust global economy. *So why can't you be a part of that transformation?*

"

A good leader inspires people to have confidence in the leader, a great leader inspires people to have confidence in themselves.
~ Eleanor Roosevelt

SUCCESS SECRETS REVEALED!

Becoming a great leader isn't an easy feat. Success frequently necessitates learning from others who have previously attained their objectives and maneuvering through the obstacles of entrepreneurship can be one of the biggest challenges that you may face on your journey to success in leadership. While leadership is indeed one of the areas that go underdeveloped by many entrepreneurs, having a mentor may be a huge help in getting you on the right path.

Here are twenty personal success secrets from seasoned business leaders who mastered the art of success and leadership.

1. Set a goal for yourself.

Richard Branson claims that his greatest motivator is to continue to push himself. He views life as a continuous university study in which he can learn new things every day. You can do it, too!

2. Do work that you are passionate about.

There's no denying that running a business takes a significant amount of time. But, according to Steve Jobs, the only way to be happy in life is to pursue work that you truly believe in.

3. Take a chance.

"Whether you think you can or think you can't, you're right," Henry Ford famously said. We never know how our efforts will turn out unless we put one foot in front of the other and take the steps. Believe in your ability to succeed, and equally as important is to have confidence in the people you lead. It is up to you to instill confidence in others by believing in their abilities and capabilities.

4. Have a clear picture of what you want to achieve.

Whether you are working solo or with your team, make sure that your vision is clearly defined and outlined. It helps a great deal when everyone is on the same page and working towards the same goal. Take time to really understand who is helping you achieve the mission by painting the picture and staying ahead of the goals.

5. Surround yourself with wonderful people.

Who you hang out with determines who you become. According to Reid Hoffman, co-founder of LinkedIn, the fastest method to transform yourself is to hang out with individuals who are already the way you want to be.

6. Confront your fears.

It is not simple to overcome fear, but it must be done. Arianna Huffington once said that fearlessness was like a muscle for her: the more she exercised it, the stronger it grew.

7. Make a decision.

Great ideas abound in the world, but only action leads to success. The simplest way to get started, according to Walt Disney, is to stop talking and start doing. That is also true for your success.

8. Keep track of the time.

No one succeeds right away, and everyone started somewhere. "If you look closely, most overnight achievements took a long time," Steve Jobs wisely observed. So don't be afraid to put effort into your business.

9. Manage your energy rather than your time.

What you can do with your time is limited by your energy, so use it carefully.

10. Assemble a fantastic team

No one succeeds in business by themselves, and those who try will always lose to a formidable team. So, to ensure your success, assemble a team that is committed to you and that aligns with your mission and purpose.

11. Hire people who have a sense of humor.

Hire for character and ideals as you assemble your crew. You can always teach someone new talents, but you can't change someone's values once they've joined your organization.

12. Make a capital-raising strategy.

"It's nearly always tougher to acquire funding than you imagined it would be, and it always takes longer," venture capitalist Richard Harroch advises aspiring entrepreneurs. So, keep it in mind."

13. Be aware of your objectives.

According to Ryan Allis, co-founder of iContact, having the destination in mind every day ensures that you're working toward it. Set goals for yourself and remind yourself of them daily.

14. Make mistakes and learn from them.

Errors, according to many entrepreneurs, are their finest teachers. Even if you initially failed, you could get closer to success by learning from your mistakes.

15. Get to know your client.

According to Wendy's founder Dave Thomas, one of the three keys to success is knowing your customer. You'll be able to give the solutions they require if you know your customers better than anyone else.

16. Take notes from your complaints.

Bill Gates famously observed that your most dissatisfied clients are your best teachers. Allow dissatisfied consumers to show you where your service is lacking.

17. Seek feedback from customers.

It's impossible to succeed by assuming what clients want or need. So instead, you must directly question them and then carefully listen to what they have to say.

18. Use your money carefully.

Make sure you spend your money carefully when it comes to your business. It's all too simple to spend too much money on dumb things and run out of money too quickly.

19. Be well-versed in your field.

"Don't play games you don't understand, even if you see a lot of other people making money from them," warned Tony Hsieh, the creator of Zappos. To be successful, you must have a thorough understanding of your sector.

20. Go above and above the call of duty.

Larry Page, the founder of Google, encourages entrepreneurs to go above and beyond what customers anticipate. It's a terrific approach to stand out in your field and gain a devoted following of supporters.

Being a successful entrepreneur involves a great deal of effort, vision, and tenacity.

"

The success of a leader is measured when one has the conviction to impart a lasting imprint in the lives of others.

~ Dr. Bonita Parker

144

Shit Great Leaders Do

A COMPILATION OF WISDOM FROM INDUSTRY GURUS

EXCLUSIVE INTERVIEW WITH CEO & BESTSELLING AUTHOR, LACHANDA WOOTEN

I had the pleasure of meeting LaChanda a few years ago at my book signing event. I will never forget the woman who stood before me – quite reserved but confident. It was something about the way you approached the table to inquire about publishing services and as I listened to you give the overview of your book, I knew big things were on the horizon for you. I am delighted that you agreed to share your success journey – the highs and lows – and ultimately all the way to the top as Managing Partner at a top accounting firm.

How did you know that you had the right idea and were people supportive of it?

As a growing and whimsical child, I was uncertain about many facets of my young life. But as I began to listen to others, especially my mom, aunties, and my teachers, I thought about, where or what does it mean?

The belief that as human being we look to attain support from family and friends through a set of doctrines, habits, and practices that which is the source of who we are in our present state of existence. Over a period, I have set out to accomplish and respond to certain dogmas, philosophies, and principles which should be accomplished. However, at the center of it all, is a relationship with Jesus Christ that increases my strength to endure. He helps and directs my relationship to achieve a goal that most may try to discredit as self-centered or selfish. I strongly believe that each person prefers or desires a growing relationship that can shape their inner-self and gather an abundance of faith along the way. One may ask, how is this achieved? Simply put it is achieved if I look at my physical being (self only), then I must draw closer to the inner spirit that seeks to enhance a positive spin on all my fallacies. Then I can grow and promote model principles based on what has allowed me to sustain a solid foundation in life. I am then able to overcome adversities and grow into perfect peace and harmony with mankind. Out of the grassroots of love, strength, and guidance, I can then be equipped to share and transfer bountiful gifts for the betterment of others.

In this second collection of my journey on this earth, I have garnered a fundamental thought that my core principle of life is based on my faith. I can climb to that mecca of inner peace and strength that so rightfully has been bestowed upon me from my humble beginning in the womb of my mother. God has given me the power and courage to move in his spirit.

With a grateful heart and peace within, I hope that you can conquer those fears and apprehensions knowing that faith is the divine source of endurance and love.

Describe some of the mistakes have you made along the way and how did you pivot?

We all make mistakes through cliques my tier level of learning from my mistakes, such as re-entering college after my first birth also, working in different careers that upon analyses were mere steppingstones but not exactly my primary choice to satisfy that thirst within. The heart listens as we walk and talk but the mind focuses on the future. I saw that what I had envisioned would take me further both financially and spiritually, then I began to move in that direction. For example, taking the time to attend evening classes while working and maintaining family responsibilities began to put me in a new direction for my career.

Quitting my full-time job was one of the toughest decisions of my life. When I got a job as a partner in one of the top one hundred firms, I was super happy. I even popped champagne with my girlfriends and family: it was the job for which I had hoped.

The moment I started things turned out very differently. Within weeks, it was clear that the job was eating up my life. I spent five days a week away from friends and family (and with my manager staying next door to me). The other two days were spent recovering, making it up to friends and my spouse for my absence, and doing my laundry and admin. I felt squeezed. Though I learned a lot about managing big projects, teamwork, and spreadsheets (an underrated superpower), I didn't really experience seeing how businesses worked from the inside as I hoped.

Through self-development books and local meetups, I started meeting more entrepreneurs and on the other, I began to think I have started my own adventure and crafting my lifestyle. When you have a salary coming in on the same day every month (or week), you have time. On one hand, that time makes you procrastinate and never pull the trigger. On the other hand, though, it allows you to think long-term and take strategic actions, rather than survival actions. As for the first time, I didn't know what I didn't know. That included how long it would take to finish the product and get the first sale in this profession and of course, I also overcomplicated things.

You don't have to replace your salary straight away, but you must create a repeatable way to generate value for others. That way, all you have to do is multiply your efforts (not find out what the formula is)

In my corporate job, I knew exactly what to do: wake up, go to the office at 9, finish my list of tasks and duties, and follow my CFO's instructions. Communicate everything clearly to my team, and you get praises and...eventually a promotion. It's not easy, but it's not complicated either. I was tired in my mind and I just didn't want to play that game. When I started a business, I had no idea what the rules of the game were.

To figure it out, it took me a few months: I read a ton of books, went to events, made mistakes, and asked other people. I could have short-cut this.

Running a business has allowed me to meet incredible people, share experiences with friends, and create interesting days outside the office which allowed me to meet more women during the week. It's also given me the growth and confidence to upgrade all my human relationships. But it did come at an initial cost. Having a business allows me to travel in 2021, I spent days abroad, vacationing in different cities (while growing and working my business). It's awesome, but it's also different from what most other people do.

When things come with benefits, like interesting experiences and stimulating friendships, it's easier to accept that you are going your own way. But when things are tough and you have to figure out a business challenge, you constantly wonder whether you made the biggest mistake of your life.

Leaving my job to start a business has been one of the best decisions of my life.

- It's allowed me to face my challenges and grow as a person.

- It's allowed me to create value for others and collect thank-you notes.

- It's allowed me to craft my lifestyle and spend months abroad each year.

- It's allowed me to connect to inspiring entrepreneurs with massive businesses.

- It's allowed me to oversee my own choices and take control of my income.

Thankfully, even some of these biggest mistakes carry valuable lessons that began to propel more energy, ambition, fun, relaxing and innovative strategies to support my need. Here again, many things that help cover and erase the mistakes, I learned in the classroom or through experiential learning in workshops, team studying while getting that motivational push from within and from family members to move further. There was a guidepost in my everyday thoughts that said, "you can do this; no matter the time, you can do it. "

What do you believe are the core qualities of a leader and why?

Finding ways to start a business can be a challenging task amid all the other things in our lives that compete for our attention. This excerpt will provide you with information and exercises that will aim to bring you closer to your goal. It will teach you skills for more effective communication and conflict resolution, and increase your passion, desire, and commitment to your dreams. In this, you will have the opportunity to complete several exercises that will give your insight into your business relationships and their strengths and weaknesses. You will also gain a better understanding of how your feelings, behaviors, and beliefs influence your network, and what changes you can make to function more effectively as a business owner. It can also serve as a resource to go back to and reference throughout your endeavors and in the future. Although there is an abundance of various books available on the topic of business, few of them provide a two-way interaction between the writer and the readers. Reading material is better and easier to process when it engages the readers in exercises that help them apply the information they have read. For example, it will provide you with the skills necessary to build a foundation for your business that will be stronger than before. It will also provide you with the tools that your relationship will benefit from if you implement them. It is important to note that building a strong relationship requires effort and work. Why am I writing this? In the last decade, a wide variety of individuals have turned to the use of self-help workbooks for assistance and treatment with a variety of problems and disorders. Such individuals have taken advantage of the plentiful resources available to care for their own struggles, whether with the help of a clinician or independently.

The core principles that I thrive and use every day is faith, hard work, and love. Always introduced as the necessary ingredients required for a healthy lifestyle, especially in the entrepreneurial world. Faith may consist of a belief that you will be able to reach your goal, a sense of confidence that this book will be able to guide you through a difficult time, or a faith that God will restore your relationship and bring about healing and restoration. The concept of work consists of the time, energy, and effort required to bring your business to the desired level. Lastly, love consists of valuing your partner and not engaging in hurtful and devaluing behaviors toward one another. This will serve as a tool to make the approach available to you in an easily accessible manner. You will be able to engage in your daily workplace at any time and place that is most convenient for you. This is the fun part.

What is the best advice that you could lend to a new/aspiring entrepreneur?

Your first business is going to take everything you've got to make it a success. You'll need your best idea, a strong work ethic, and perseverance for those days where things just don't go your way. But that combo can help you turn your simple idea into an empire.

The best boss I've ever had once told me that her secret to building a productive team centered around making her employees happy and never listen to others that do not have the best interest. And it was true. For many years there was a celebration of some kind in the office all the time. I literally cried because I didn't want to leave. Also, if I had listened to a few people that made statements of, "you're leaving the government," and "um you're crazy" I only left because I knew I had to step out of my part-time tax office job and gain more impactful accounting experience.

I worked in that role for seventeen years, that's how long-lasting the impact of employee morale is. Unfortunately, it's often the one thing entrepreneurs fail to focus on. Most first-time entrepreneurs try to act like a boss. And no employee wants one of those. Your employees want to feel appreciated, heard, and know that they're on the right track. If you find yourself constantly criticizing people for not doing it your way, you'll often find that team performance will drop. The most important business tip when it comes to managing employees is to make them happy. Because if you do that, they'll be more willing to help you hit your company's goals.

Everyone wants to have some elements of power in their lives. But figuratively speaking we all have some power. Power is that gift to create things unimaginable by others. It is the cornerstone to success. It is the building block upon which we can see closure to gain insights into the struggle of others. It can be the here and now tools upon which we climb to the highest peak or mountain on earth or diving into the deepest depth of ourselves and make it happen.

The unparalleled power of God provides a spiritual understanding that from birth we can live to eternity. If we claim this unparalleled power of God, then we know that victory is yours.

LaChanda Wooten is a dedicated worker that promotes and encourages punctuality, academic acumen, organizational processes, and aptitude in a collegiate work environment. She is driven by her wholesome relationship of a wife/helpmate, a caring and loving mom, a devoted sister, and the impressive legacy to which that of her mom and grandparents passed down through a generation of inheritance.

LaChanda currently serves as the Managing Partner in one of the top 100 Accounting firms in Maryland. My past experiences were a significant source of my will to do more. I served for 17 years in the DC Government as Senior Project Director in the Title III Office of the University of the District of Columbia, Washington, DC. With over 25 years of project management leadership, on and off-site event planning skills, interior, and design decorating crafts as her passion, she indulges the boldness of personal workmanship and craftiness with a dedicated spirit to support her clientele. These qualities are symptomatic of many positive results that have promoted more interest from friends and business partners across the board.

As a career goal and interest of LaChanda, she was motivated to pursue the ladders as a successful African American female. She has earned an Associate Degree in Business, a Bachelor of Science degree in Business Administration, a Master's in Business Administration, and a second Masters' degree in Business Science Administration with a concentration in Human Resources. While moving the needle forward, she is a candidate for the Doctoral Program at Regent University and pursuing the title of Enrolled Agent to add to the many facets she thrives for every day.

She is, nonetheless, a business owner, an entrepreneur that is devoted to her craft, her children, and seeks to be an exceptional and dedicated/hardworking woman while maintaining her creative skills and dedication to the God she serves.

"

*Don't let the noise of others'
opinions drown out your
own inner voice.*

~ Steve Jobs

JOURNEY TO SUCCESS

by Dr. Shannon D. Howard

As a therapist and entrepreneur, I often get asked, *"How did you do it? How did you achieve success and become a leader in your industry?"* When I sat to think of how to answer this question, simple answers came right away. There are many things that make an outstanding leader, but there are things one must do to achieve success in a leadership role. I will expound on specific things that I did before expanding my private practice into a group practice.

I knew that to be an outstanding leader, it was important to be well-versed in a variety of areas to develop my communication and leadership skills. It was equally imperative that if I wanted to be an effective leader, it took listening to those who were willing to serve and help grow my business; but for them to be successful at serving me, I had to share my vision with them and seek others who could be an asset to my company if partnering was an option. Vetting ... vetting ... and more vetting of partners was essential – but before I go on, let me give you some insight.

The Journey Begins

I was never a stranger to entrepreneurship and business ownership. I guess you can say it was in my blood. When growing up, we often discussed entrepreneurship as it pertained to my extended family. My father shared stories of my grandfather, who was a sharecropper who owned his own farm, tended to animals for food, and owned the surrounding land. My grandfather owned several properties across acres of land in North Carolina where his children benefited from his legacy. Although both of my parents worked great government jobs, they too, have several properties that are willed to our family as their legacy. Most recently, we (parents and siblings) have talked about owning a commercial building, which we all could leave for the next generations of the Howard family. Although we are in the talking phases of this plan, I anticipate investing in this project shortly.

Throughout my college years, surprisingly, I did not plan to be in business for myself. My plan was to work with a hospital facility or a mental health clinic where I could use my doctorate in the areas of assessment and psychological testing. Despite those plans, I learned in my mid-twenties that working for others would not work well for what I had planned. It wasn't until I was abruptly fired that I decided and learned how to build a clientele for myself to start my solo practice while contracting with several agencies within the community.

When I initially shared the news with my parents that I was going into business for myself, they had minor reservations because it was not something I had done before. I was totally dependent, with no financial cushion to fall back on. Thankfully, contracting allowed me to build my practice separately while also keeping my bills paid. Despite their concerns, they encouraged me to try it. Fortunately, my parents were supportive and have always taught me and my siblings to be financially independent. Call it blind enthusiasm, but either way, I was excited about getting the ball rolling. I was nervous when starting out. I began submitting claims to insurance companies and stalked my mailbox daily as I waited for insurance claims to be paid in time for bills. My parents taught me early the importance of saving money for a rainy day, which helped when claims were delayed. Contracting with a group nearby also afforded me the luxury of having another stream of income.

Working as a contractor opened more possibilities for greater exposure for building my private practice. I established my home office in 2003. Once I got my state provider number, I sought new clients, learned the billing system, and scheduled my first client. While working as a private practitioner and contractor, I learned how to get credentialed with more commercial insurance companies. This was essential because it gave me more credibility and exposure in health care insurance directories.

Overcoming the Obstacles

Starting a new business had its obstacles. For many years I went without insurance because of insurance restrictions during those times. Although I could afford to go to the doctor if I needed to, being without health insurance was a tremendous risk. I paid out of pocket for physicals, medication, and eye exams. As a private practitioner early on, I also went without a 401k plan, life insurance and worked often since I got paid only when I worked. *These are some of the things that most new entrepreneurs don't consider.*

I saw obstacles as temporary. I was willing to sacrifice and be frugal so that bills stayed paid. And although I was late at times on minor bills, I prioritized what was reported to the credit bureaus – those got paid first, while utilities such as gas, phone, water, or electric were paid partially or late. I recall a few rare occasions when a utility (gas and water) was cut off for a day or two until claims came in. I did not reach out to my parents for help since I had a plan and could manage the inconvenience of a temporary utility off for a short while. *Talk about small sacrifices.*

Bills weren't the only things that I had to sacrifice. Vacations with family and missed opportunities to travel in the beginning phases of starting my private practice were also on the roster. In 2005, I returned to school to get my doctorate. Because school was a top priority, I sacrificed more to manage school and work balance. *Being in business requires sacrifice.* There were times when money flowed in heavily, while changes to my schedule could significantly affect revenue. I relied on credit cards and made minimal payments in the early phase of business ownership but still managed to make extra payments when I could.

This experience was a genuine test of my faith, patience, and resilience. *I never gave up!* There were many times I was frustrated and weary about the process that I endured. I learned that persevering was key to anything worth holding on to and fighting for. I set my mind to a certain outcome and did not give up until I reached my goal. *And that's what entrepreneurship is about!* I continuously challenged myself – even to this very day – to keep moving forward, no matter what, by reciting mantras to get me through. My go-to's were from *The Secret* by Rhonda Byrne, *"Act as if it's impossible to fail," and" keep your thoughts on the best possible outcomes."*

I believe one of the most challenging things about entrepreneurship was knowing when and how to pivot as obstacles arose on my journey. Don't get me wrong – I am a "pick-myself-up and dust-me-off" type of girl, but that doesn't mean that the fear didn't exist. A good lesson to learn on your road to success and becoming a great leader is to not be afraid to fail and expect mistakes along the way! If the goal is the same, nothing should keep you from it. You do not have to know it all but know who to go to for answers. Reach out to colleagues or other industry leaders that you trust and who are available to consult with you when needed. There is no need to reinvent the wheel. Others have created businesses before you and paved the way for you to learn from.

When overcoming obstacles, find people who you can rely on for inspiration and motivation. Recognize that minor obstacles come with being successful but there are always solutions, especially if you trust colleagues who also want to see you thrive.

Continue to seek supervision from those who have been successful in business longer or who can suggest options you had not considered. To be successful in business, one's mindset must focus on making things happen or finding alternative solutions to achieve the desired goal. Accepting failure (if it happens), but also being willing to push forward and continue is what sets successful leaders apart.

Making the Vision a Reality

For years I saw expanding my private practice into something bigger and better. I tried to build with partners, but for many reasons, it did not work. Once I realized what criteria my business partner needed to possess, I became more selective about who was a better fit. *Don't just settle for anybody as your partner.* It is important to note that I considered several partners early on, but we were not a good fit in business. I often shared my dream with friends from school and finally, my best friend talked to me about possibly joining together to start a group practice that would offer a variety of services that would change our industry for decades to come. We met several times a month and mapped out our vision and goals.

We agreed that reaching out to other industry consultants in the local area would give us a greater perspective to help us prepare to pitch our business plan. We researched free local resources to gain insight into important questions. How would we form? What locations would be ideal? What finances would we need? How to develop an impressive business plan, and are we aligned with the right person for this long-term commitment? Lastly, what would we do if a partner decided to dissolve their partnership? All these things are vital when you are looking at bringing a partner to help you carry out your dream.

I was both nervous and excited as I began exploring the answers to these questions. We both enrolled in business classes to learn the ins and outs of forming and marketing our company. We learned about other professionals in the area who provided consultation services on accounting, book-keeping, and legal matters. Once we had the basics in place, we mapped out the vision for our company by developing two to three vision boards that highlighted in depth what we hoped to achieve in the first 3-5 years. Although astronomical, we developed confidence in our ability to build a thriving practice in which we would create our vision and bring it to life. *You must have a clear, concise vision for the business you are trying to build. It gives you something to work towards so that you aren't wasting time doing tasks that do not lead you towards your highest goal.*

Notable Business Start-Up Tips

One of the key elements to consider when establishing a joint venture partnership is to make sure that you trust the partner or partners you select. It would behoove you to be clear about what you need in a partner by devising criteria that each partner needs to possess to be considered for the partnership. For instance, know the educational background history of the person; the prospective partner's work ethic/history; tax and creditworthiness, and other pertinent information that helps in deciding if the partnership is a great fit. Discuss openly what happens if either partner wishes to dissolve the partnership. I strongly suggest utilizing a business attorney for this process.

My journey individually was interesting. Another essential factor to consider during the planning phase of starting any business is family support. My life partner was essential in meeting each group of partners I considered, and he took an active role in our commercial property searches. Learning how to separate one's ego to hear wise advice is a hurdle I went through over the years in my quest for business partners. My initial vision started in the early 2000s, but the time was not ideal due to school obligations. I considered several other partners, and although they all thrive in their individual practices as professionals, establishing a great fit was a challenge. I noticed my pattern of taking on the bulk of responsibility and feeling more motivated than my counterparts. Although it may not have been a lack of motivation, results showed that the right people, place, and time, had to be aligned for a solid foundation and growth.

Different personalities and workflow can make or break the success of any business. Learning how to communicate issues or problems before they develop into bigger concerns should be a daily practice. This also means that being open to criticism, suggestions and new perspective should also be at the core of business development between partners as they work alongside each other. My business partner and I do not always have to see eye to eye, but we agree to hear each other out and bring any topic to the round table to sort through. When we agree to develop each other's ideas, we devise a practical plan to determine when new ideas will be implemented. If we cannot agree, we use our business consultants as a platform to gain greater perspective before making major changes that may not be cost-effective or could be detrimental to our business reputation.

Speaking of which, having an excellent reputation goes a long way when starting a new business. My business partner and I left a successful group practice and maintained relationships with colleagues that we can consult and refer clients between each other. Having a good moral compass and exercising in abundance versus lack creates a pathway for a business to thrive. Instead of seeing colleagues as competitors, we see other providers as an extension of our support system. There is more than enough to go around and we are eager to refer clients to other providers if we are not knowledgeable in a modality or specialty.

Learning from the Mistakes

In any business, learning from mistakes helps to prevent challenges in the future. We will never know everything because it is impossible to know what you don't know. When situations like this arise, make notes, and aim to prevent the same mistake twice, if possible. One situation that instantly comes to mind is when we were doing the paperwork for the practice, we needed to have an address to start the credentialing process. Determining an address was easy, but we learned later in the process that we needed an actual lease versus a simple address prior to, which could've been a major setback. Constant changes with credentialing and insurance companies remain a challenge if you do not have adequate knowledge and support staff to tackle these issues daily. Being able to have a collaborative relationship with other businesses that aid in the daily function of the business is necessary for your business's success.

Overall, when considering a new business, research, research, research. Ask as many questions as you can to those who are in the same industry. Research your demographic area early on. Before signing a lease check with your local planning and development office to make sure you can operate your business within the leasing space of your choice. Take classes yearly to learn about changes within a business or consult with business professionals who will work with you to stay abreast of frequent changes to tax law and policies. Develop your business plan in depth to reflect the roles of each person in your business and projections as your business grows. Research what systems you will need so that your business flows daily. Learn from your mistakes. Be kind to yourself when you find you don't know something. What you don't know, seek answers from resources around you. Take breaks when needed outside of daily self-care routines. Love what you do and do what you love. Be willing to teach others who reach out to you for guidance. Past the torch and help others thrive as well.

The Importance of Self-Care

During the COVID pandemic, my business partner and I endured a few challenges that caused us to move our entire practice to an online tele-mental health platform, which differed vastly from our face-to-face contact with clients. It was during this time that we had to lean on and consult with other outside colleagues about what platforms they used and why. Outside of work, we relied heavily on each other for moral and emotional support due to our steady level of friendship. We were able to have tough conversations whenever necessary and attack conflict head-on because of the relationship we'd built over the years.

Early in my journey into entrepreneurship and building a thriving group practice, I've learned the importance of establishing self-care routines when things become stressful and overwhelming. *Trust that things will come up! No business that I've seen has been "thing-proofed."* Things will always come up at the most inopportune moment, which is simply the nature of business. During these times, be sure to take care of YOU by incorporating daily breaks throughout your day. Also, vacations or mental health days are necessary and should be implemented into your schedule. *Make time for yourself.* We owe it to ourselves to be mentally and emotionally healthy and sound for our clients. In order to serve them, we must meet our needs daily to ease burn-out or fatigue.

Dr. Shannon Howard is a highly sought-after professional counselor and CEO of SinClair McCoy, LLC. She serves as a sexual relationship specialist who focuses on assisting women and men with healing from childhood trauma surrounding sexual abuse. Her extensive educational background consists of dual degrees in both Counseling and Clinical Psychology with a focus on Philosophy and Women's Studies. She also possesses specialized training in trauma with clients who require treatment in the areas of sex offenders and survivors of sexual assault.

She believes every client is unique in their own way and that each person's story is different. This is the catalyst behind her Pleasure Principle, a coaching method that encompasses the 4 Rs to recovering from past sexual trauma. Using targeted strategies and a personalized coaching approach, she creates a platform that not only increases the awareness of sexuality but also assists couples and individuals transition from victim to victor and face their past trauma head-on by uncovering and resolving the root issue, assess desired outcomes, and implement a plan of action that helps them build healthy, solid intimate relationships.

She is the author under the alias SinClair McCoy of The Alternative book trilogy.

To connect with Dr. Howard, please visit:

www.sinclairmccoybooks.com

174

IT WAS ALWAYS THERE

by Jamboa Renee Davis

I knew early in life that I wanted to be a BOSS. I was extremely smart, very interested in finances, business, working for myself, and always wanted to be in charge of everything even as a young child. My mom used to tell me all the time that you are going to be something special and help me when you get older. I remember growing up and everyone around me would say that I was going to grow up and be a doctor, lawyer, or teacher; I knew they were wrong and way off base. I was a natural-born leader and too head-strong for my own good most times. I remember one of my schoolteachers asked me what I wanted to be when I grew up. I looked her in the eyes and said, "I want to own my own business." That one moment in my life sent me on a serious mission and journey towards achieving success in entrepreneurship and caused me to try about every single pyramid scheme known to man ... problem was, I was no way a salesperson and ended up wasting a lot of time, money, and effort. I soon realized that what I did have, however, was a strong gift of gab and had the keen ability to shift the narrative of any situation using my own unique voice. And knowing now what I wasn't sure of back then, was that gift would be the secret sauce to my success journey.

Discover Your Why

Knowing the reason behind why we do something major in life is by far one of the most essential elements of achieving success in life. It gives meaning to the things that we desire most and is the deciding factor in whether we give up or continue pushing forward.

I remember when I was growing up, my mother would always encourage me to speak up and express myself, no matter what. So, it was no surprise to her when I pivoted and later developed a strong desire to become a lawyer. Immediately out of high school, I became somewhat of a "serial educator" and developed this urge to know and learn all that I could. Still unsure of the exact direction I wanted to take in life, I enrolled in the law program at Howard University Saturday College and shortly thereafter, received my certificate in Behavioral Social Science. As if that wasn't enough, I enrolled at Bowie State University where I was certified in Microsoft Applications. I continued my educational journey getting certified in almost everything I could, yet still feeling like something was missing.

By this time, my youngest daughter was turning one and my oldest daughter was completing her last year of high school. I was ready to take on everything that came my way. But I could not ignore the stirring in my soul to have my own business and work for myself. I needed and wanted to start a business and leave a legacy for my girls; that was the most important thing to me. After all the time I'd wasted feeling dissatisfied with the direction that I was taking my life professionally, I knew that I wanted a better alternative for them – a better example of what success looked like. They were my "why" and every choice, action, and sacrifice that I made was so they could have a better life.

Discover Who You Are

Knowing who you are at the core, is another key element to achieving success. It is the very thing that separates the leaders from the followers, and the haves from the have nots. And I was determined to, in no way, be the latter.

I was in my thirties with a personality that could shake any room up when I walked into it because I knew my shit. I was confident and my aura spoke for itself. I decided to go after a job with a well-known construction company and after interviewing with the most intriguing woman I've ever met; I got the job! And ultimately, she would play a huge role in who I am today.

I started the job in an entry-level position and, after 16 years of being with the company, I had managed to work my way up the ladder and was eventually offered a promotion as Controller and Acting CFO of the company. It wasn't easy especially working as a young black woman in a male-dominated industry. But I worked hard and was determined to earn a good living and use this as my steppingstone to fund my big dreams.

Little did I know, a curveball would be thrown at me that I never saw coming ...

Learn to Pivot

This step in the process is known as the "make or break" of a lot of entrepreneurs. There will always be roadblocks and curveballs thrown at you when you are on your way to something big, but you must learn how to think on your feet and shift gears – even when you never see it coming. As the saying goes, "the devil is always busy," especially when you are on your way to the top!

Shortly after making my mark in the company that I had come to love, things shifted. A new guy was hired as the Chief Financial Officer and it dampened what I had thought was the ideal working environment. He was an egotistical nightmare and tried to corrupt everything I implemented and critiqued every idea that came across his desk from me. He was old fashion and stuck in the 1970's accounting era. The morale in the office shifted to an unhappy place to work. I soon realized if I didn't make a move, I was more than likely going to be fired. And there was no way that I was going to stand for a "Johnny-come-lately" to change the dynamics of my work environment or threaten the position that I had worked so hard for in the company.

I remember going home and sitting with my parents – explaining the situation at work. We talked and prayed, and I knew deep down I had to make a quick decision ... the right, quick decision, which would work in my favor and would make me feel worthy and not worthless; one that would propel me and not stifle me. Let me tell you - prayer truly works.

I remember it like it was yesterday, August 21, 2011. I decided that after sixteen years on a job that built someone else's dream, working hard, long hours just to endure what I had been inadvertently forced to put up with, I quit! I walked away from it all and never looked back.

For two months after leaving that job, I sat around watching Maury – trying to figure out what my next move would be, and then it hit me. I realized that what I had done for that company, I could certainly do for myself. I had the skills, knowledge, and expertise to make it happen. So, I launched my own accounting firm, Jamboa Davis LLC. What was astonishing even to me, was that within two months, I had acquired my contracts and made more money working three days a week than I had working a fifty-hour work week for someone else. This revelation only increased my desire to have more. I wanted more because I knew I deserved more and was fully capable of achieving more. Now, let me let you in on something that shouldn't have made a difference ... but when God is in the midst, for those who believe and for those who love Him, He will take an average day and turn it into a marvelous moment.

Learn to Leap

As an entrepreneur, next to being able to pivot, I believe that taking fast action also plays a part in whether you are successful or not. Successful entrepreneurial leaders are doers. They can spot a potential opportunity in just about anything – if there is one to find. The key is that when the opportunity is placed in your face, you must recognize it and immediately act on it. Great opportunities don't always come around twice – remember that!

I remember my mother and I used to ride around just looking at neighborhoods, houses, and businesses. It was a "thing" that we simply loved doing. One day, we were riding down Benning Road S.E. in Washington D.C. and saw a local barbershop with a "for sale," sign in the window. As quickly as my mind processed it, I immediately saw a potential opportunity for not only me to open a storefront shop, but also to help my little brother expand his business as well. After consulting with a friend and my parents, I decided to buy it.

I just leaped! I wasn't letting that opportunity slip through my fingers.

When I signed the contract, I later found out there had been ten other applicants all bidding for the same property. But for some reason, GOD blessed ME with the opportunity. I sealed the deal in December of 2011 and became the proud owner of Unique Cutz Barbershop located on Benning Rd. SE Washington D.C. Three years later, *you guessed it,* I opened Unique Cutz 2, located in Forestville Maryland, the second location in growing my barbershop chain. It was not easy at all but I was faithful to the empire I wanted to build.

Seize the Opportunity

After achieving success with the barbershops, I still had that fire inside of me that just wouldn't quit burning. I knew I would become unstoppable in my pursuit of the so-called "American dream."

I remember being in the office one day crunching numbers when my former boss piqued my interest during a conversation by saying "hey why don't you get your own trucks, have your own trucking company; you know the entire business of running a construction company." I had not thought of that before that moment but I was certainly intrigued by the seed that he had planted. It's not every day that someone in the same field or business would encourage you to become their competition. I viewed this as a sign – a golden opportunity that I could not pass up on. So, I leaped … again.

After a few months of doing research and implementing my plan of action, I became the owner of Traffic Jam LLC., a dump truck company.

Always Stay Gracious and Humble

The worst thing you could do or be – as an entrepreneur – is arrogant with a chip on your shoulder. Know that in business, no matter what the industry is, there will always be someone who does you wrong; there will always be someone who doesn't like you; there will always be someone who may not agree with your ways of doing business. However, one thing for sure is that there will always be people who cannot deny your talents and your zone of genius. Stay true to who you are and what you bring to the table and those same people who were against you just might be placed in your path looking for your help. As Beyonce would say, "always stay gracious – the best revenge is your paper!"

In 2014, I had been hired to do some accounting work for the construction company where I had once been employed. Go figure! Now the Bible teaches us that God will prepare a table before us in the presence of our enemies. Please believe it. While I did not consider my previous employers my enemies, I must admit it felt good knowing they still needed me and my expertise, which put me in a position to name my price and leverage the opportunity as a contractor.

Four years later, I opened my third barbershop and this time, I focused on hiring mostly women and building a full-service beauty spa specializing in hair, nails, skin, makeup, body contouring, and women's wellness.

Build a Solid, Sustainable Brand

If you ask any successful entrepreneur how they made it in their industry through all the ups and downs – and the highs and lows, I guarantee you they would say two things: unwavering faith and the fact that they built a solid business that they could scale. Every business brand should have, at minimum, three to five ways to generate revenue. So, if you have an idea, make sure you can carve out ways to make money from it so that if one slows down or halts, you still have two more to keep your revenue flowing. After all, the average millionaire has at least seven streams of income …

During the excitement of expanding my beauty and spa business and putting together beauty workshops, the pandemic hit and I was forced to shut down all three of my barber/beauty shops due to the COVID pandemic. No one saw it coming! Who would have thought in my lifetime that I would be living through a worldwide pandemic? For an average entrepreneur, this should have, could have been completely devastating. Don't get me wrong, I was scared, confused, and devastated because the shops that I had worked so hard for were now closed for something that was completely out of my control. I remembered thinking, "What is going to happen to all my businesses." So many people didn't build a business that could weather a storm like this – they didn't have multiple streams of income or sustainability in their industry. I was counting my blessings that I was one of the ones who did. *AMEN!*

I knew deep in my heart that I wasn't going to fold, falter or lay down because that wasn't what my mother raised me to do, that's not who I am. Faith walks with me. When things seem to go left in business; you must have a plan, a vision, determination to move forward. I worked with management to come up with a plan for both Barbershops because they were already solid, established businesses. So, I decided to revamp the new business, the spa. The one business that burned a hole in my pocket for a year until I produced a new plan. That's what living the life of an entrepreneur is, adjusting and surviving.

I could have let the space go, but there is something special about this place so I carved out ways on how it would bring me revenue and sustain in its industry. I got the master plan and decided to turn it into an event venue for patrons to rent out to host events and business workshops, and I plan on offering classes and services of my own

Thinking business and doing business are two different things.

As for the spa, no worries there! I was able to secure a smaller, more eloquent space for both women and men to come and get pampered. This full-service wellness spa (Unique Xperience Spa) is an extension of Unique Cutz.

Also, during the pandemic, I decided to step outside of my comfort zone and try my hand at something very new to me. I decided to do a spirit brand. I had thought of launching a tequila brand for a while but never took action to bring it to fruition. I didn't know much of anything about the industry, I did my research to acquire all the appropriate paperwork, sought out a distillery, and took my time building the brand for my premium vodka. The whole experience was interesting and exciting and very personal to me. I wanted to honor the woman who had given me so much and who was gone too soon. Only a handful of family and friends knew what I was up to because I intended to surprise my dad with a finished bottle because the entire process of creating it had everything to do with my lovely mother, Ethel Delores Callahan.

E'thal56 Vodka would become the name.

The vodka's name E'thal56 after my late mother Ethel Callahan who passed away from cancer at the age of fifty-six. The colors of the bottle purple and silver had been her favorite colors and represent royalty. The numbers fifty-six was her age at the time of death but was also the year she was born. The entire concept of E'thal56 was created in remembrance of my mother's legacy. She was a phenomenal person who loved to bring everyone together especially her family. E'thal56 represents her life and now when we get together celebrating and having a good time, she will be there in the midst.

I remember holding the finished product in my hands and giving it to my dad who had no idea what I had been up to. He held the bottle and a smile was so big came across his face as he looked at me and said, "Your mother would be so proud of you." At this moment, I knew my vodka brand was going to do great and this is just the beginning of something more marvelous to come. Today, E'thal56 Premium Vodka can be purchased at eight liquor stores in the Washington, DC metropolitan area within its first 4 months of launching.

Two barbershops, one trucking company, one wellness spa, one event center, and a vodka spirit brand ... not bad for a woman who started with a little bit of faith and a big dream from uptown Washington, DC.

... and I'm just getting started!

Final Words to New and Aspiring Entrepreneurs

Success can be a scary thing but if you keep the faith and have the knowledge you need to accomplish your goals, you will succeed.

I'm proud of what I've accomplished yet humbled that God placed me in the right place at the right time and for such as time as this. Now, I want you to know that the mind of an entrepreneur never stops, never rests and we spend a great amount of time thinking, planning and plotting. As an entrepreneur, you must have a vision, passion, confidence, and motivation.

Don't wait to live the life you want. Look in the mirror and take some self-inventory, make the decision to live with confidence and resilience. This journey isn't for the faint of heart. You must be willing to face your fear and leap despite the obstacles you will face, and go out on a limb because, in fact, that's where the fruit is.

Make the sacrifices you need to make to become the leader that is nestled inside of you. Become a sponge and take the time to learn everything you can about your industry, its competitors, and its alliances. Do your research, ask questions, and never be embarrassed by the mistakes you'll make because those same mistakes are what will allow you to become better. Don't become complacent, have a plan, and create a strategy then light the match and set it on fire.

Entrepreneurship is not and will never be all glitz and glam. I worked hard; very hard; and continue to work hard to keep every damn business I have launched and in success mode. There will be times when you want to give up, times where you'll be confused about what to do. You may even doubt yourself and wonder if it's worth the headache. *My answer is YES!*

On your journey, you won't need confirmation from others to become successful. There will be nay-sayers and dream-killers coming from every angle, but don't succumb to their tragedies. Surround yourself with like-minded people who want what you want, success. Don't be dismayed by the fact that everyone will not support your vision; it's YOUR vision for a reason and you can keep it alive by implementing and executing your plan of success.

Be the leader that is not afraid to break the rules and take control of their destiny. *Anything is possible when you believe in yourself.*

Meet Jamboa "Renae" Davis – serial entrepreneur, mother of two daughters, and mega-influencer in the Washington D.C. metropolitan area. Her background lies in small business consulting and accounting services in the beauty and fashion, health and wellness, entertainment, and transportation industries. Her passion is to continuously motivate and encourage entrepreneurs, women, and young adults globally by providing resources and tools that aid in their success.

In addition to her entrepreneurial endeavors, Renae serves as the Vice President of Diamonds Star Divas, a 501c (3) organization that hosts charitable and community service activities and events that embodies empowerment, encouragement, self-awareness, productivity, and positivity through bonding in sisterhood.

She received several business certifications and undergraduate degrees from Howard University, Bowie State University, and Prince Georges Community College. During her downtime, she loves to travel with family, read novels, write, and listen to music.

To connect with Jamboa Davis, please visit:
www.jamboadavis.com

"

The only things you can change permanently are the hearts of the people you lead.

190

CONCLUSION

The legacy of a leader is fostered by his or her own personal values. We live in such a *"what can you do for me"* world that people tend to forget about what they can and should do for others, that, eventually, will continue well after they have left the earth. It's a powerful reminder that true legacies live through people, not results. And having a positive impact will ripple far beyond your tenure when you connect, develop, and inspire.

One of the primary reasons I invested time into authoring this book is so that successful leaders are reminded of what it means to be a great leader and to build relationships and accomplish something memorable that will help individuals move forward long after they are gone. The greatest legacy any successful leader can leave is having developed other leaders. I began my entrepreneurial journey over 15 years ago, and in the last few years, I've begun to personally invest in coaches and aspiring authors who are actively seeking to teach others the values and principles I embrace. I smile at the revelation that the impact that I've had in their lives was enough for them to instill in those individuals seeking to learn from them.

I'm sure you have heard that "when the student is ready, the teacher appears." Well, this is also true that when the teacher is ready, the student appears. There are people in this world who would be honored to learn from you—not just the person who will succeed you in your leadership position, but people in every area of your life. So, when someone crosses your path with the sole purpose of becoming better than they were the day before, nurture them. Give them your fuel so that they too, can make it to the top. Be patient, work hard, keep your eye on the ball, and keep learning, and you'll eventually achieve the success you desire and become the leader that you were meant to be.

In the words of John Maxwell, "Achievement comes to people who are able to do great things for themselves. Success comes when they lead followers to do great things for them. But a legacy is created only when leaders put their people into a position to do great things without them."

“

The legacy of successful leaders lives on through the people you touch along the way.

Dr. Bonita Parker

APPENDIXES

195

196

New SWOT Analysis

This framework recognizes that threats and opportunities can be both external and internal, and that they can be shaped by your strengths and weaknesses and the strengths and weaknesses of others.

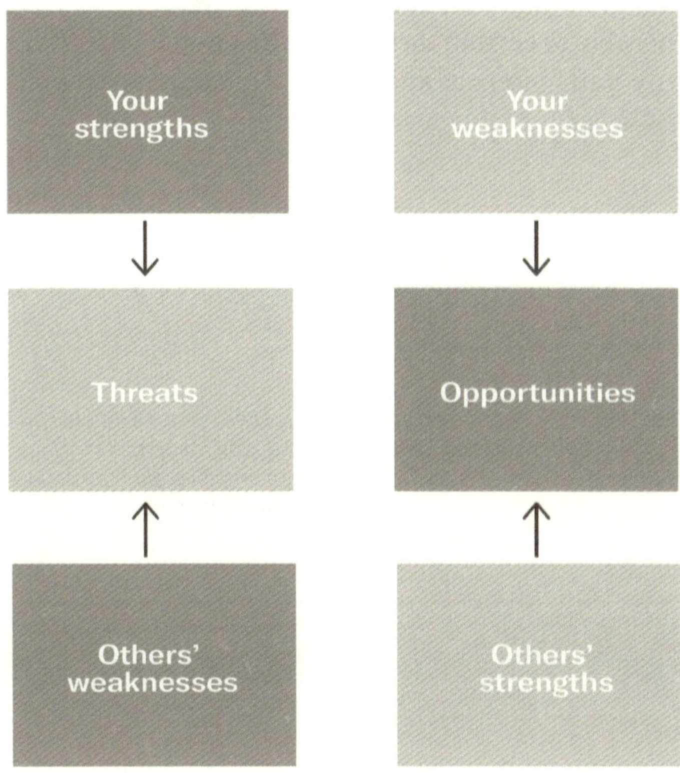

Source: Adam Brandenburger   HBR

Personal SWOT Analysis

A personal SWOT analysis can be useful for reaching a personal goal, improving performance at work, applying for a new job, or other situations requiring an honest and detailed look at what factors may be supporting you or holding you back. Your strengths may lead you to opportunities, while your weaknesses could make you vulnerable to certain threats. Use this personal SWOT template to identify your internal and external resources as well as weak spots and areas for improvement.

INTERNAL FACTORS	
STRENGTHS (+)	**WEAKNESSES (-)**
Talk about what you're good at, your unique assets and resources, and how your positive attributes are perceived by others.	*Talk about improvements you need to make, any resources you lack, and how these negative attributes might be perceived by others.*

EXTERNAL FACTORS	
OPPORTUNITIES (+)	**THREATS (-)**
List doors that are currently open to you, opportunities you can capitalize on, and how your strengths can create new connections.	*List any harmful hazards, competitors, and how known weaknesses can open the door to threats.*

Self-Assessment 1: Value Systems

Rank the values in each of the two categories from 1 (most important to you) to 5 (least important to you).

Rank	Instrumental Values	Rank	Terminal Values
____	Ambition and hard work	____	Contribution and sense of accomplishment
____	Honesty and integrity	____	Happiness
____	Love and Affection	____	Leisurely Life
____	Obedience and duty	____	Wisdom and maturity
____	Independence and self-sufficiency	____	Individual dignity
____	Humility	____	Justice and fairness
____	Doing good to others	____	Spiritual salvation

Scoring Key: The values that you rank highest in each group are the ones that are most important to you. Consider whether your actions, career choices and so forth are consistent with your values.

Source: Based on C. Anderson, *"Values-based management,"* Academy of Management Executive 11, no.4 (1997); 25-46; M. Rokeach, *Beliefs, Attitudes, and Values* (San Francisco: Josey-Bass, 1968).

Self-Assessment 2: Emotional Intelligence

Indicate whether each of the following statements is true or false for you.

Self-Awareness

______ 1.   I am aware of how I feel and why.

______ 2.   I understand how my feelings affect my behavior and my performance.

______ 3.   I have a good idea of my personal strengths and weaknesses.

______ 4.   I analyze things that happen to me and reflect on what happened.

______ 5.   I am open to feedback from others.

______ 6.   I look for opportunities in perspective.

______ 7.   I put my mistakes in perspective.

______ 8.   I maintain a sense of humor and can laugh about my mistakes.

______ 9.   I can stay calm in times of crisis.

Managing Emotions and Self-Regulation

______ 10.   I think clearly and stay focused when under pressure.

_______ 11. I show integrity in all my actions.

_______ 12. People can depend on my word.

_______ 13. I readily admit my mistakes.

_______ 14. I confront the unethical actions of others.

_______ 15. I stand for what I believe in.

_______ 16. I handle change well and stay the course.

_______ 17. I can be flexible when facing obstacles.

Self-Motivation

_______ 18. I set challenging goals.

_______ 19. I take reasonable and measured risks to achieve my goals.

_______ 20. I am results oriented.

_______ 21. I look for information on how to achieve my goals and improve performance.

_______ 22. I go above and beyond what is simply required of me.

_______ 23. I am always looking for opportunities to do new things.

_______ 24. I maintain a positive attitude even when I face obstacles and setbacks.

_______ 25. I focus on success rather than failure.

_____ 26. I don't take failure personally or blame myself too much.

Empathy for Others

_____ 27. I pay attention to how others feel and react.

_____ 28. I can see someone else's point of view, even when I don't agree with them.

_____ 29. I am sensitive to other people.

_____ 30. I offer feedback and try to help others achieve their goals.

_____ 31. I recognize and reward others for their accomplishments.

_____ 32. I am available to coach and mentor people.

_____ 33. I respect people from varied backgrounds.

_____ 34. I relate well to people who are different from me.

_____ 35. I challenge intolerance, bias, and discrimination in others.

Social Skills

_____ 36. I am skilled at persuading others.

_____ 37. I can communicate clearly and effectively.

_____ 38. I am a good listener.

_____ 39. I can accept bad as well as good news.

_______ 40. I can share my vision with others and inspire them to follow my lead.

_______ 41. I lead by example.

_______ 42. I challenge the status quo when necessary.

_______ 43. I can handle difficult people tactfully.

_______ 44. I encourage open and professional discussions when there are disagreements.

_______ 45. I look for win-win solutions.

_______ 46. I build and maintain relationships with others.

_______ 47. I help maintain a positive climate at work.

_______ 48. I model team qualities such as respect, helpfulness, and cooperation.

_______ 49. I encourage participation from everyone when I work in teams.

_______ 50. I understand political forces that operate in organizations.

Scoring Key: For each of the fifty items, give yourself a 1 if you marked "true" and 0 if you marked "false". Consider your total for each of the subscales and your overall total score:

Self-Awareness:	_________	out of 8
Managing Emotions:	_________	out of 9
Self-motivation:	_________	out of 9
Empathy for others:	_________	out of 9
Social Skills:	_________	out of 15
Overall total:	_________	out of 50

Those with higher scores in each category, and overall, demonstrate more of the characteristics associated with high emotional intelligence.

Source: Based on information in D. Goleman, *Working with Emotional Intelligence (New York: Bantam Books, 1998)*

Self-Assessment 3: Type A Behavior Pattern

Indicate whether each of the following statements is true or false for you.

Self-Awareness

______ 1. I am always in a hurry.

______ 2. I have a list of things I have to achieve on a daily or weekly basis.

______ 3. I tend to take one problem or task at a time, finish it, then move to the next.

______ 4. I tend to take a break or quit when I get tired.

______ 5. I am always doing several things at once both professionally and personally.

______ 6. People who know me would describe my tempura as hot and fiery.

______ 7. I enjoy competitive activities.

______ 8. I tend to be relaxed and easygoing.

______ 9. Many things are more important to me than my job.

______ 10. I really enjoy winning both at work and at play.

______ 11. I tend to rush people along or finish their sentences for them when they take too long.

______ 12. I enjoy "doing nothing" and just hanging out.

Scoring Key:

Type A individuals tend to answer questions 1, 2, 5, 6, 7, and 10 as true and questions 3, 4, 8, 9, and 12 as false. Type B individuals tend to answer in the reverse (1, 2, 5, 6, 7, and 10 as false and 3, 4, 8, 9, and 12 as true).

Self-Assessment 4: Locus of Control

Read the following statements and indicate whether you agree with Choice A or Choice B.

	A	**B**	
1.	Making a lot of money is largely a matter of getting the right breaks.	Promotions are earned through hard work and persistence.	______
2.	I have noticed a direct connection between how hard I study and the grade I get.	Many times, the reactions of teachers seem haphazard to me.	______
3.	The number of divorces indicates that more people are not trying to make their marriages work.	Marriage is largely a gamble.	______
4.	It is silly to think that one can really change another person's basic attitudes.	When I am right, I can convince others.	______
5.	Getting promoted is really a matter of being a little luckier than the next person.	In our society, a person's future earning power depends on his or her abilities.	______
6.	If one knows how to deal with people, he or she is really quite easily led.	I have little influence over the way other people behave.	______
7.	The grades I make are the results of my own efforts; luck has little or nothing to do with it.	Sometimes I feel I have little to do with the grades I get.	______

8. People like me can change the course of world affairs if we make ourselves heard. | It is only wishful thinking to believe that one can readily influence what happens in our society at large. | ———

9. A great deal that happens to me is probably a matter of chance. | I am the master of my fate. | ———

10. Getting along with people is a skill that must be practiced. | It is almost impossible to figure out how to please some people. | ———

Scoring Key: Give yourself 1 point for each of the following selections: 1B, 2A, 3A, 4B, 6A, 7A, 8A, 9B, and 10A. Scores are interpreted as follows:

> 8-10 = High internal locus of control
> 6-7 = Moderate internal locus of control
> 5 = Mixed
> 3-4 = Moderate external locus of control
> 1-2 = High external locus of control

Source: Adapted with permission from Julian B. Rotter, "External Control and Internal Control," Psychology Today, June 1971: 42. Copyright by the American Psychological Association.

Self-Assessment 5: Narcissism

For each of the following statements, indicate the degree to which you think each describes you by writing the appropriate number. For example, if a statement fits you well and sounds a lot like you, you would write 4.

4 = Sounds a lot like me/fits me well
3 = Sounds like me
2 = Does not sound like me
1 = Does not sound like me at all/does not fit me at all

_______ 1. I see myself as a good leader

_______ 2. I know that I am good because everyone tells me so

_______ 3. I can usually talk my way out of anything

_______ 4. Everybody likes to hear my stories

_______ 5. I expect a great deal from other people

_______ 6. I am assertive

_______ 7. I like to display my body

_______ 8. I find it easy to manipulate other people to get what I want

_______ 9. I don't need anyone to help me get things done

_______ 10. I insist on getting the respect I deserve

_______ 11. I like having authority over other people

_______ 12. I enjoy showing off

_______ 13. I can read people like a book

_______ 14. I always know what I am doing

_______ 15. I will not be satisfied until I get all that I deserve

_______ 16. People always seem to recognize my authority

_______ 17. I enjoy being the center of attention

_______ 18. I can make anybody believe anything

_______ 19. I seem to be better at most things than other people

_______ 20. I get upset when people don't notice or recognize my accomplishments

_______ 21. I enjoy being in charge and telling people what to do

_______ 22. I like to be complimented

_______ 23. I can get my way in most situations

_______ 24. I think I am a special person

_______ 25. I deserve more than the average person because I am better than most

_______ 26. I have a natural talent for leadership

_______ 27. I like to look at myself in the mirror

_______ 28. I know how to get others to do what I want

_______ 29. The world would be a better place if I were in charge

_______ 30. I am going to be a great person

Scoring Key:

Desire for power and leadership: add up scores for 1, 6, 11, 16, 21, and 26. Total: _______

Need for admiration and self-admiration: add scores for 2, 7, 12, 17, 22, and 27. Total: _______

Exploitiveness: add scores for items 3, 8, 13, 18, 23, and 28. Total: ________

Arrogance and a sense of superiority: add scores for items 4, 9, 14, 19, 24, and 29. Total: ________

Sense of entitlement: add scores for items 5, 10, 15, 20, 25, and 30. Total: ________

Add up the total for ALL five subscales: ________ (120 highest possible score).

Interpreting Your Score: The five subscales are the key factors in narcissism. The highest possible total in each subscale is 24, with the highest possible total score of 120. The higher your scores, the more narcissistic characteristics you have. Some degree of narcissism is associated with healthy self-esteem and effective leadership.

Source: Based on Emmons, 1987: Raskin and Terry, 1988, Rosenthal and Pittinsky, 2006.

Self-Assessment 6: Views of Power

This self-assessment is designed to provide you with insight into your attitude regarding power. Indicate your opinion on each question, using the following scale:

5 = Strongly disagree
4 = Somewhat disagree
3 = Neither agree nor disagree
2 = Somewhat agree
1 = Strongly agree

_______ 1.　It is important for a leader to use all power and status symbols that the organization provides in order to be able to get his or her job done.

_______ 2.　Unfortunately, for many employees, the only thing that really works is threats and punitive actions.

_______ 3.　In order to be effective, a leader needs to have access to many resources to reward subordinates when they do their job well.

_______ 4.　Having excellent interpersonal relations with subordinates is essential to effective leadership.

_______ 5.　One of the keys to a leader's influence is access to information.

_______ 6.　Being friends with subordinates often reduces a leader's ability to influence them and control their actions.

_______ 7.　Leaders who are reluctant to punish their employees often lose their credibility.

_______ 8.　It is difficult for a leader to be effective without a formal title and position within an organization.

_______ 9.　Rewarding subordinates monetarily is the best way to gain their full cooperation.

_______ 10.　In order to be effective, a leader needs to become an expert in the area in which he or she is leading.

_____ 11. Organizations need to ensure that a leader's formal evaluation of their team is actively used in making decisions about them.

_____ 12. Even in most enlightened organizations, a leader's ability to punish subordinates needs to be well preserved.

_____ 13. The dismantling of formal hierarchies and the removal of many of the symbols of leadership and status caused man leaders to lose their ability to influence their subordinates.

_____ 14. A leader needs to take particular care to be perceived as an expert in their field.

_____ 15. It is essential for a leader to develop loyalty to subordinates.

Scoring Key: Reverse score item 6 (1 = strongly agree, 5 = strongly disagree), then add your scores on each item as follows:

Legitimate power: add up scores for 1, 8, and 13. Total: ______

Reward power: add scores for 3, 9, and 11.   Total: ______

Coercive power: add scores for items 2, 7, and 12. Total: ______

Referent power: add scores for items 4, 6, and 15. Total: ______

Expert power: add scores for items 5, 10, and 14. Total: ______

Interpreting Your Score: Your total in each of the preceding five categories indicates your belief and attitude toward each of the personal power sources available to leaders.

Self-Assessment 7: Authentic Leadership

Being an authentic leader consists of several different elements. For each of the following items indicate to what extent the statement is descriptive of you, using the following scale:

1 = Strongly disagree
2 = Disagree
3 = Agree
4 = Strongly agree

______ 1.   I am aware of who I truly am.

______ 2.   I know what matters to me most.

______ 3.   I make my decisions based on my own principles, rather than what others think.

______ 4.   I have trouble handling my weaknesses and faults.

______ 5.   I have trouble opening up to others.

______ 6.   When I am in groups, I like to share as much information as possible with everyone.

______ 7.   Although I respect others' opinions, I tend to stick to things I believe in.

______ 8.   When I get conflicting advice, I have trouble deciding what the best course of action may be for me.

______ 9.   I am skilled at listening to and understanding many different points of view.

______ 10. I like to hear information from all sides before I make up my mind.

______ 11.   Most people don't really know who I am.

______ 12.   I can tell when I am not being true to myself.

Scoring Key: Add up your rating for all 12 items. The maximum score is 48. A higher score indicates behaviors that build credibility.:

Self-awareness: add up scores for 1, 2, and 12. Total: ______

Balanced perception: reverse score for item 4 (1=4, 2=3, 3=2, 4=1) and add scores for 4, 9, and 10. Total: ______

Value-based behavior: reverse score for item 8 (1=4, 2=3, 3=2, 4=1) and add scores for items 3, 7, and 8. Total: ______

Relational transparency: reverse score for item 5 and 11 (1=4, 2=3, 3=2, 4=1) and add scores for items 5, 6, and 11. Total: ______

Add up the total of all four subscales: ______

Interpreting Your Score: The range for the total scale is between 12 and 48. The closest you are to 48, the more elements of authentic leadership you have. Consider each of the subscales (scores range from 3 to 12) for areas where your score may be lower.

Source: This self-assessment is based on work by Kernis (2003) and Avolio and Gardner (2005).

Self-Assessment 8: My Personal Mission Statement

One of the most important aspects of leadership development is self-knowledge and awareness of your priorities and values. You can use the information in Self-Assessment: Values to review your values and keep those in mind as you complete this exercise.

Step 1: What Do I Want to be When I Grow Up?

What do I want to be known for?

If there was one thing I would like people to remember me for, what would that be?

What should my epitaph say about me?

When I retire, what I would like my most important accomplishment to be?

Step 2: My Personal Mission

Based on the results of the self-assessment about values, and the answers to the questions above, write your personal mission statement. There is no right or wrong answer!

For a step-by-step tutorial on developing your personal mission statement, based on Franklin Covey principles, see https://msb.franklincovey.com/. Or once you have developed your mission statement, keep it accessible. It can guide you when you are having trouble making decisions and in setting the path for your development as a leader.

MEET THE AUTHOR

Dr. Bonita Parker is an experienced and certified Master Life Coach, CEO Success Coach, Publisher, and 3x international bestselling author who is the driving force behind the success of Bonita Parker Enterprises, a multifaceted corporation that strategizes with new and aspiring business leaders to identify their core strengths, build out their individual success blueprint and provide resources that get excellent and proven results in their business.

Dr. Bonita knows firsthand the importance that authenticity and transparency can have when building a thriving business and has dedicated her time to helping women break through emotional barriers and mental blockages that hinder their success. Under the tutelage of her **Dream Achievers University (DAU)**, a virtual certification academy that focuses on the study of life coaching. she has helped a multitude of clients across a wide range of personal development sectors step into the light of entrepreneurship and build successful brands using her personal **Radical Success Brilliance Model**. Using this interactive step-by-step methodology, clients are able to break free from invisible enemies, shift their mindset and align with their optimal success path.

She has been featured in many publications including Black Enterprise, Essence.com, Chicago Tribune, Atlanta Journal, SHEEN Magazine, HuffPost, and FOX34.com to name a few, and is the recipient of several prestigious honors.

2019 – Woman of Achievement Award
2019 – Entrepreneur of the Year
2019 – Mentor of the Year Award
2019 - Strength, Courage & Wisdom Honor
2018 – Author Academy Award Nominee
2017 – Woman of the Year Award
2017 – Anthology of the Year Honor
2016 – Woman on Fire Award
2015 – Metro Phenomenal Woman Award

Her motto *"Get Radical"* has gained national attention and serves as the catalyst behind her core messaging. She consistently motivates and inspires others to live out their life bold and free from fear by staying true to who they are, being completely authentic, and using transparency to gain the trust of those they wish to serve.

223